Don't Just Do
Something, Sit There

Also by Sylvia Boorstein

It's Easier Than You Think: The Buddhist Way to Happiness

Don't Just Do Something, Sit There

A Mindfulness
Retreat with

Sylvia Boorstein

HarperSanFrancisco
An Imprint of HarperCollins*Publishers*

HarperSanFrancisco and the author, in association
with The Basic Foundation, a not-for-profit organi-
zation whose primary mission is reforestation, will
facilitate the planting of two trees for every one tree
used in the manufacture of this book.

A TREE CLAUSE BOOK

HarperCollins Web Site:
http://www.harpercollins.com

HarperCollins,® ▟® HarperSanFrancisco,™ and
A TREE CLAUSE BOOK® are trademarks of Harper-
Collins Publishers Inc.

FIRST EDITION

Library of Congress Cataloging-in-Publication Data
Boorstein, Sylvia
    Don't just do something, sit there : a mind-
fulness retreat with Sylvia Boorstein. – 1st ed.
    ISBN 0–06–061252–5 (pbk.)
    1. Meditation–Buddhism.   2. Spiritual life–
Buddhism.   I. Title.
BQ5612.B66   1996
294.3'443–dc20   95–32865

96 97 98 99 ❖ RRD(H) 10 9 8 7 6 5 4 3 2 1

In appreciation of mindfulness,
and with gratitude for the
opportunity to practice, this book
is dedicated to you, the reader.

May your practice thrive.
May we all wake up.
May all beings be happy.

Contents

Day Three: Going Home Day   *127*

Acknowledgments

All of my students, by sharing their practice with me, helped me become a teacher. I am grateful to them. My friend Martha Ley helped me prepare the manuscript with an acute critical ear and an absolutely uncritical heart.

Thank you, Martha.

PART ONE

Preparing
for the Retreat

Don't Just Do Something, Sit There

When I was offered the opportunity to write this manual, I was delighted. Worrying arrived one moment later. "Uh-oh," I thought, "a manual usually prescribes things to do. Can I possibly say, 'Don't just do something, sit there?' "

I began to think of Buddhist rituals I know. Certain practice lineages contain ceremonies, prayers, and chants, quite lovely ones. Just as soon as I remembered them, though, I put them aside. In mindfulness practice, the only thing we add to current experience is calm attention.

Mindfulness, seeing clearly, means awakening to the happiness of the uncomplicated moment. We complicate moments. Hardly anything happens without the mind spinning it up into an elaborate production. It's the elaboration that makes life more difficult than it needs to be.

I discovered my habit of transforming neutral fact into painful opinion many years ago when I phoned a monastery to arrange to do a private retreat. The person I spoke with said, "You need to talk to Robert, the retreat master." I left a message for Robert and was assured he would call me back. The following day I had a message on my answering machine from Robert saying he was returning my call. The day after that, I phoned and was told, once again, that Robert wasn't there. I explained that I had called Robert and Robert had called me and here I was, now, calling Robert again. I added, embroidering the situation, "Maybe this is a sign that I'm not supposed to do my retreat there." The response I got was, "I think it's just a sign that Robert isn't here." I had complicated my moment.

Mindfulness practice is the habit of seeing things in an uncomplicated way. You do not need to wait until a retreat time to start practicing. Nor do you need to go *away* to do your retreat. If you can easily negotiate a supportive retreat space, that's great. It *is* helpful to be away from familiar diversions and to have some seclusion. But if going away is not an option, you can do a retreat at home by ignoring familiar diversions, unplugging the phone, and posting a sign: "Three-Day Retreat in Progress."

Retreat practice starts before the retreat. It begins with the *decision* to practice, with the intention to be mindful. You have already started.

Cosmology Is Optional

You can practice mindfulness without any concern about compromising your religious beliefs or affiliations. It *is* true that the Buddha had a cosmology that might be different from yours, and it *is* true that the Buddha taught mindfulness as a main practice, but he didn't teach that cosmology and mindfulness were interdependent.

One famous Buddhist story describes a novice monk complaining to the Buddha that he had not been given enough cosmological answers. (Imagine! Complaining to the *Buddha*!) In the story, the Buddha agrees with the novice but says that intellectual formulations are not what end suffering. To illustrate this point, he gives a hypothetical example in which a person shot with a poisoned arrow discusses the particulars of the shooting before having the arrow removed. Removing the arrow, not discussing the shooting, is the way to address the person's suffering. A contemporary Buddha might use the example of a person who is injured in an accident, then whisked away by paramedics to an emergency room. The injured person does not stick around to discuss the particulars; the police can do that. Directly addressing the suffering is clearly the wisest response.

The Buddha taught that mindfulness is the direct antidote to suffering because it leads to wisdom. I like to think of mindfulness practice as a way of becoming wise *and* being wise at the same time.

The *becoming wise* part is a gradual process. By paying attention calmly, in all situations, we begin to see clearly the truth of life experience. We realize that pain and joy are both inevitable and that they are also both temporary. We remember, more and more often, that struggling causes suffering and that compassionate, considered responses make life manageable. Sometimes we forget. The long-term goal of practice is to never forget.

The *being wise* part of mindfulness practice happens as we act now, in this very moment, on the way to never forgetting. Mindfulness practice cultivates the habit of not getting angry with life because it isn't happening in the way we'd like. Unpleasant situations call for balanced responses. Anger is extra. Mindfulness practice also cultivates the habit of enjoying pleasant experiences while they last without lamenting their passing. Camera film ads notwithstanding, we cannot capture the moment. Mindfulness practice means *acting* as if we were already enlightened.

"Nobody's Grandmother Is a Buddhist"

My friend Jean told me that she had discovered a large hornets' nest under the eaves of her roof. Her eight-year-old granddaughter, Courtney, who was with her at the time, was frightened and didn't want to stay outside. Jean, too, was dismayed by the presence of so many hornets and paused to consider possible remedial alternatives.

Sensing her grandmother's reluctance to take immediate action, Courtney asked, "What are you waiting for?"

"I'm thinking," Jean replied. "I don't like having these hornets here either, but Buddhists don't like to harm living beings . . ."

Courtney looked up at Jean with the sideward, skeptical look children have when they think someone might be teasing them. Finally, she shook her head in disbelief. "Naah," she said. *"Nobody's* grandmother is a Buddhist."

I think what Courtney meant was, "Hey, you can't change cultural contexts on me all of a sudden!" Practicing mindfulness does not mean becoming a Buddhist. It means living like a Buddha.

Why Meditate?

The Buddha didn't teach very much meditation. Mostly, he taught about suffering. He showed how the mind becomes confused and fatigued chasing pleasant experiences and running away from unpleasant experiences. Pleasant and unpleasant experiences, the joys and pains of everyone's life, are not, he explained, the problem. It's the chasing and running that creates tension in the mind. That tension is what the Buddha called suffering.

Some people, when they heard the Buddha teach, understood him so completely that all their mind habits of chasing and running (which are called *clinging* and *aversion* in formal scripture language) stopped forever. They were called *arahats*–fully enlightened beings. For everyone else, the Buddha taught special practices.

The principal meditative practice the Buddha taught is called *mindfulness*: relaxed, nonclinging, nonaversive awareness of present experience. You could think of it as a natural capacity that, like any other skill, requires developing. A retreat provides a special opportunity to practice.

The instruction manual that the Buddha wrote for mindfulness practice is a sermon called "The Foundations of Mindfulness." I reinspire myself each time I read the opening paragraph: "This is the sole way . . . for the overcoming of sorrow and lamentation, for the destroying of pain and grief." That's *such* an exciting possibility.

The rest of the sermon is the Buddha's instruction guide for the four ways to pay attention. This manual, like the Buddha's, will include all four of these methods in what is, basically, a practice of attentive sitting and alert walking.

Mindfulness is like other skills that become effortless and automatic with practice. I can knit and think at the same time, without dropping stitches. My friend Alta used to be able to knit in the movies. At the beginning of meditation practice you need to *remember* to be mindful. After a while, you can't forget.

But Why Do a
Meditation *Retreat?*

Since mindfulness practice is a way of being in the world rather than a specific technique that can only be practiced on certain occasions, being on retreat seems extra. If alert, balanced presence in our lives is the goal of practice, why not practice in the midst of life rather than in seclusion?

There is a good reason. Of course the truth is available in every moment, and we could wake up to wisdom and freedom in the supermarket as well as on a meditation cushion on a retreat—but a retreat is different. There are no diversions. There is nothing to entertain ourselves with. Since there is no place to hide from ourselves, there's a good possibility that we will know ourselves better after a retreat than we did before.

But self-knowledge is only the beginning. Liberating understanding comes more from seeing how *things* are than how *we* are. Seeing the truth of the cause and the end of suffering begins to allow us to live more freely. Being alone, with no diversions, sets up ideal conditions for beginning to see.

My motivation for going on my first mindfulness retreat was my husband's enthusiasm. He returned from his first ten-day practice period and said, "Syl, this is great.

You should do it." Some months later, I was enthusiastically describing my own retreat experience to a friend, probably emphasizing the rigorous schedule and Spartan regimen. That part didn't impress him. He responded to my story by saying, "I can't believe you sat alone with your mind for two weeks!"

Nothing marvelous or dramatic happened to me during my first retreat. No exotic mind events happened at all, nor did I have any particular insight about anything. For the most part, I struggled with confusion and sleepiness, and my body was in pain. It was hard for me to concentrate. I didn't quite understand what *mindful* meant. But I was totally captivated by the teachings I heard about suffering. If, in this very life and in this very body, peace of mind was a possibility, I was quite prepared to sit alone with my mind.

The schedule in this manual is planned for a three-day retreat. It is expandable to accommodate a longer retreat. Repeat Day Two for every extra full day of practice. Then follow the schedule for Day Three on going-home day, even if it falls on Day Seven.

Regardless of the length of your retreat, the final instruction will always be "Now, go home and continue being mindful forever."

Keep
Everything
Simple

All the *complicated* activities of a mindfulness retreat happen before the retreat begins. If you are going away, you need to arrange for a place to stay. Ideally, it would be someplace quiet and free of distractions, but it need not be remote. A cabin in the country would be wonderful, but a quiet midtown hotel room would work. In addition, there are retreat centers and monasteries throughout the country where individuals can arrange to do solo meditation practice. Retreatants may have the choice of taking their meals with the resident community or being served separately. At some centers, retreatants stay in cabins with cooking facilities and prepare their own meals.

Even if you are just going around the corner to a cottage in a friend's backyard, there will be certain logistics to deal with. You need to reserve your space, perhaps arrange for travel, pack, change your phone message, take your cat to the cat-sitter–whatever your particular responsibilities are, you need to delegate them. If you can arrange in advance for your meals to arrive at scheduled intervals, that would be great. If you plan to prepare them yourself, keep the meals simple. Keep *everything* simple. Keeping the retreat externals very plain allows the responses of the heart and mind to show up in sharper detail.

The less we elaborate on our outside experience, the more tuned in we become to our inner experience. Suppose you went to the theater, and just as the curtain rose, a team of carpenters armed with pneumatic drills started to renovate the backstage dressing rooms while the Rose Bowl Parade passed by in the street outside. You would have trouble staying focused, and the play would not make sense.

When we are able to watch our experience in detail, we see clearly the internal ping-pong of the mind as it goes about liking or not liking every single thing. Until the game itself becomes clear, there is no possibility of knowing that options to it exist.

Paul Revere had the words "Live Contented" inscribed on the wedding ring he gave to his wife. It sounds like an instruction, hardly the sort of romantic declaration usually associated with wedding rings, but I think it is a *great* wedding gift. I wish someone had told me, long before I learned it from the Buddha, that contented living is a *choice*.

Take a
Minimum
of Stuff

Mary's Mantra

The *least* challenging thing about preparing for a mind-fulness retreat is the packing. Take the normal necessities that you would for the same number of days spent any-where—clothes to keep you warm (or cool) enough, a comb, a toothbrush, soap, toothpaste—the minimal per-sonal hygiene equipment that is standard issue for nuns and monks. Don't bring books, other than this manual. Leave your journal at home. You don't need your Walk-man. To make it easy for you to follow the schedule, bring a timer that has a pleasant ring. You don't need anything else.

Years ago I was having lunch in my kitchen with my friend Mary. We were teaching a class together that after-noon, and with our habitual, under-the-wire approach to teaching, we were making our lesson plans as we ate. At some point, one of us realized it was time to leave. We scrambled into our sweaters, gathered up our books and papers, and started out the door.

"Wait a minute!" I said, as I glanced down at the pile of stuff I was carrying. "I don't think I have everything I need."

"Sweetheart," Mary replied in her voice of absolute authority, "You are *never* going to have everything you need!"

Mary's mantra has been a great support to me through twenty-five years of classes. I have repeated it to myself innumerable times as one of the focusing and calming practices I do just before I am about to teach. I *could* have planned more, *could* have researched more, *could* have brought more stuff along. But I always teach anyway. I manage with what I have.

It's the same with life. We certainly could have been better prepared. Mostly, we do it without an instruction manual. Mostly, it's a surprise. It's usually what happens when we are planning something else. Maybe it's *always* what happens when we are planning something else. We manage anyway. Practicing mindfulness is practicing managing gracefully.

So pack minimally. There is always *something* you could have taken along that would have enhanced your experience: a warmer sweater, a sweeter-tasting toothpaste, a firmer meditation cushion, an extra shawl. This feeling is a natural response to the truth that it's hard to keep the body comfortable. Left on its own, it runs out of steam. The body needs a certain amount of ongoing attention to maintain its comfort level, and we often have the notion that if we get it a little *more* comfortable, it will stay that way longer. It might, but it would be just a *little* longer, and in the long run we would just be delaying the real work of mindfulness practice, which is accommodating the heart to change.

Mindfulness itself is portable and invisible.

Go.

"It's Only a Weekend"

Think of mindfulness as "hanging out, happily." Don't expect a radically altered mind state—unless feeling happy and relaxed is radical for you. Happy and relaxed *probably* will happen. Healing from particular heart wounds might *begin* to happen. But having an agenda adds unnecessary and unrealistic complexity to what should be simple.

I recall beginning a weekend of retreat practice many years ago and passing my teacher Jack Kornfield in the hallway during the pre-retreat, settling-in stage of Friday afternoon. I must have had a particularly determined look on my face, because after we had passed each other, Jack came back after me and tapped me on the shoulder. "Relax, Sylvia," he said, "it's only a weekend."

This caution doesn't mean abandoning hope that a healing perspective, even a *profoundly* healing one, might arrive during a weekend. A new and liberating view can come any time, even in this very moment. It just means "Don't plan for any *particular* result." Who knows what new view is just around the corner? Being on the lookout for something specific might divert us from seeing something really great. The mind has an incredible knack for taking care of itself. Practicing mindfulness gives it the time and the space it needs.

PART TWO

Day One

· ·

Arrival Day

Schedule for This Retreat

Day One: Arrival Day

Late afternoon: Arrive, unpack. Become familiar with your surroundings. Arrange your sitting space–cushion or chair. Find indoor and outdoor walking spaces, eat supper.

Evening: Sit–Refuge/Reflection

Walk

Sit–Instructions

Late tea

Go to bed

Day Two: Full Day of Practice

7:00 A.M.   Wake up, dress, sit until breakfast

7:30   Breakfast

8:15   Sit

9:15   Walk

10:00	Sit
11:00	Walk
12:00	Lunch
2:00	Sit
3:00	Walk
4:00	Sit
4:30	Walk
5:00	Dinner
6:00	Interactive Meditative Dharma Talk
7:00	Walk
8:00	Sit
9:00	Late tea

Day Three: Going Home Day

7:00 A.M.	Wake up, dress, sit until breakfast
7:30	Breakfast
8:15	Sit–Precept Reflection
	Informal lovingkindness practice
	Formal lovingkindness practice

I have two encouraging inner voices that support me during my retreat practice. One is my locker-room-coachin-the-halftime voice, which says, "Go for it, Sylvia. Try very hard. You *can* do it." The other is my grandmother's voice, which says, "You're doing fine. There is no way you can make a mistake. Have some tea."

The have-some-tea part of me thinks about adding to the schedule some tempering provisos: "For however long you decide to . . ." or "If you feel like it . . ." or "If you want to . . ."

But I don't believe this is the most helpful approach. There is a rationale behind the schedule. It has worked for lots of people. It is good to start with the intention to keep as close to the formal schedule as possible. But remember, whatever happens, you're doing fine. And if things become difficult, have some tea.

Unpacking

When students arrive at a meditation center, they normally spend some time getting established and settling into the rhythm of the place before sitting down on their meditation seat. Do that in your retreat place, taking as much time as you need. Otherwise, sitting practice will start with freeway consciousness or workday consciousness. Gearing down is itself a practice.

Unpack, or walk around and become familiar with your surroundings. Don't be in a hurry to get started on the *real* practice. This *is* the real practice. Not hurrying, giving full attention to each small moment, is both the technique of practice and the goal of practice.

I've noticed license plate frames that say "I'd rather be sailing" or "I'd rather be bowling." Sometimes I think it's fun to see the rather-be-doing frames because they are a hint about the driver. Other times I start reflecting about the fact that preferring to be doing something else always diminishes the present moment. I imagine starting a business that produces license plate frames that read "I'm totally content right now."

Take care of last-minute logistics. Do one thing at a time. Unplug the phone. Unpack happily. Live contented.

Refuge Reflections

Formal mindfulness retreats begin with the recitation of the formal Buddhist refuge vows, which are

> *I take refuge in the Buddha;*
> *I take refuge in the dharma;*
> *I take refuge in the sangha.*

Sit in a comfortable position. Relax. Close your eyes. Think about all the circumstances that have led you to do this practice and all the people who have made it possible for you to do this retreat. When I say, "I take refuge in the Buddha," I think, "I feel very encouraged that Siddhartha Gautama, a human being just like myself, figured out a way to live this very life, in which pain and loss are unavoidable, without suffering. He woke up; I can, too. He became free. I can, too." That thought inspires me.

When I say, "I take refuge in the dharma," I think, "I'm so glad that the Buddha taught *techniques* for waking up and that he told them over and over to people who passed them on for generations until someone wrote them down so that I can learn them now." Thus I am not obliged to reinvent the wheel. I get to use a twenty-five-centuries-tested product as a guide.

When I say, "I take refuge in the sangha," I think about my family, which has always supported my meditation practice, at home and away, and my friends, who cheer me on. Even when I do a solo retreat, I never feel alone. It pleases me to visualize the people near and far who I imagine are supporting me while I practice, and it delights me to dedicate my practice to their well-being as well as to my own.

If practice can be done on behalf of all the beings I know, it is one small step (and a very exciting one) to assume, as Buddhists do, that we practice on behalf of all beings everywhere. A classic way to begin or end a practice period is to say the following words:

> *May I be peaceful;*
> *May I be happy;*
> *May all beings be peaceful;*
> *May all beings be happy.*

Walking with
Fresh Eyes

Take a walk, outdoors or in, whatever seems best, on a route that goes somewhere but that isn't directed. In other words, don't decide where the turnaround point will be before you start out. That way, the walk can be an unfolding surprise. See everything with fresh eyes.

Suzuki Roshi, a wonderful Japanese Zen teacher who established the San Francisco Zen Center, described "beginner's mind" as that capacity of mind which is able to experience each moment as entirely new. He said that this element of expectant interest inclines the mind toward understanding. I think what Suzuki Roshi meant is that our vision is limited when we become habituated to seeing life a certain way, and that limited vision is what keeps truth hidden from us. He urged meditators to approach each practice session with the eagerness and hope that characterized their first session.

I remember Frederick Spiegelberg, when he was a professor emeritus in the Stanford religion department, describing his own first intimation of religious awareness. "I was a young boy," he said, "perhaps three or four years old, and I was at home with my mother in our second-floor apartment in the middle of Frankfurt. My mother and I were looking out the window, down into the street where there were trees and people and street cars and busyness. My mother's face was suddenly pensive, awestruck, and she said to herself, quite softly and earnestly, '*Was gibt das alles?*' [What does it all mean?]"

At least eighty years had passed since the moment when Professor Spiegelberg's mother had seen an ordinary, thousand-times-seen-before scene with eyes of wonder, but as he described it, it felt as though, for him, it had happened yesterday. I thought about his long and distinguished career as a religious philosopher, and I wondered how much of it had depended on that one instant of sharing his mother's moment of clear seeing.

Robert Louis Stevenson wrote,

> *The world is so full of a number of things,*
> *I'm sure we should all be as happy as kings.*

Babies are interested in everything. Toddlers love colorful toys, but they also love to bang on pot covers with wooden spoons and empty the contents of their mother's wallets on the floor. When Collin, age five, went with me to the Oakland Coliseum to see his first professional baseball game, he was as interested in the tires stuck in the mud flats along the bay and the tall condominiums in El Cerrito en route to the stadium as he was in the game. He was seeing everything with fresh eyes.

A meditation retreat is an opportunity to see *everything* with fresh eyes. In mindfulness practice, because we don't add anything, because the entire arena of practice is the interaction of the mind with whatever each moment brings, there is no possibility of being fascinated by novelty. Novelty is fun, but it soon becomes un-novel. What we are hoping to develop is a mind that is fascinated by *life*.

Go for your walk now. Walk for as long as you like, depending on your energy. Tomorrow, I'll add formal walking instructions that will focus attention on sensations you feel in your body as you move. For this period, let your attention rest on your new surroundings. Walk with "beginner's mind." See everything with fresh eyes.

Instructions and
Helpful Hints

I went on my first mindfulness retreat when I was forty years old, and I was self-conscious about being the oldest person there. Many of the other meditators were just back from Asia. They ate their salad with chopsticks and were clearly more "hip" than I was. Most of my current teaching colleagues were meditating in Asian monasteries while I was reading *Good Housekeeping* and the *Ladies' Home Journal* in Topeka, Kansas.

When I began teaching mindfulness, I made a deliberate effort not to sound like the "Helpful Hints from Heloise" column in my women's magazines, even though I *think* in that idiom:

"If grape juice spills on the tablecloth, pour vinegar on it immediately and launder it as soon as possible in cold water."

"If the distracting dramas of your life keep disrupting your composure as you meditate, pick out one single, plain meditation object, like your breath, and focus only on that."

"If you are *so* focused on one single, plain object, like your breath, that you become somnolent and foggy-minded, then focus on your *whole* body and its *variety* of interesting sensations, so your attention stays alert."

Hints *are* helpful. Once, when my teacher Sharon Salzberg was giving me some instruction—"Do more of this" or "Do less of that"—I said, "It feels like I'm constantly *tinkering* with the mind."

"It's *all* tinkering," she replied.

Think of it in terms of tinkering toward that balance of vigilance and composure which provides the ground from which insight and wisdom develop. Instructions, technical hints, are the *tools* of practice—not the practice itself. When people ask me what my spiritual path is, I tell them I'm practicing being wise and compassionate. When they ask "How?" I give them helpful hints.

Instructions for Sitting
Meditation Practice

Choose a sitting posture that is comfortable for you. You can sit on a chair, on the floor on a meditation pillow, or anyplace else where you can be relaxed and still stay alert. Some people even meditate on their bed, sitting propped up with pillows. Find a position appropriate to your physical abilities.

Once you've settled down into your seated posture, take a moment or two to *just* settle down. I try to sit up straight, with my spine erect, but then I allow my body to drape itself naturally and easily around me. I imagine my body hanging around my skeletal form in much the same way a soft wool coat hangs down from a firm hanger in my closet.

Let your eyes take in the scene around you, and then let them gently close. If you can, smile. It helps the mind relax. Then just sit there. Don't *do* anything. Sounds will come and go. Thoughts will come and go. You can feel where your body is without seeing it, because sensations of tingling, pressure, vibrations, and pulsings move in and out of your awareness. The Buddha called all the physical sensations of the body the First Domain or the first realm for developing mindfulness. In the Foundations of Mindfulness instructions, he suggested using body sensations as the best arena for beginning to practice.

Pretty soon, if you just sit there, the sense of your breathing will present itself to you. It might show up as waves of shifting movement in your belly. It might appear as alternating pressures around your rib cage. You might feel it as tiny flutterings in and around your nostrils. You might notice your breath as the echo of sensations throughout your body every time breath passes in and out of you. Wherever you notice it, in whatever form the breath presents itself to you, stay right there. Let your attention rest in the movement of the breath. When your attention wanders away from the breath–and it surely will!–bring it back to the breath and rest there again.

Decide before you sit how long you'll sit. Thirty minutes is good for starting.

Start now.

Question

*I'm confused! I thought you said mindfulness
meditation was a general awareness practice. I thought it was paying attention to
everything. Now I hear that I'm supposed to
stay just with the breath. Haven't you con-
tradicted yourself?*

That's a great question! It certainly *sounds* like I contra-
dicted myself. Mindfulness is, indeed, composed, alert,
moment-to-moment recognition of *all* experience, and
lots of stuff is always happening. Thoughts are continually
coming and going. Body sensations—all varieties: pulsing,
throbbing, tingling—are busily becoming perceptible and
then disappearing. Moods and emotions are pushing one
another in and out of the mind. The evaluating capacity is
clicking—"pleasant" . . . "unpleasant" . . . "I like this experience" . . . "I don't like this experience"—with every new
appearance, no matter how small it is. Experience is *very*
complex, even when we are sitting still, quietly, with our
eyes closed.

That's why we start with resting in the breath. You
might want to consider the practice of trying to rest the attention exclusively in the breath as "Remedial Mindfulness" on the road to "Regular Mindfulness." Think of it as
the warm-up exercise. What you are trying to do is condi-
tion the mind to be able to stay steady and clear with

whatever experiences arise. If you wanted to juggle eight flaming bowling pins, like the Flying Karamazov Brothers, you'd practice with the pins for a long time before you set them on fire. And you'd probably start with just two. That's why we start with just the breath.

The Easiest
Instructions of All

I heard the most straightforward instructions for sitting practice from Ajahn Amaro, a Buddhist monk who teaches mindfulness. He said, "Let the body assume its natural ease. Let the mind assume its natural ease. Now, just stay alert to anything that arises to disturb that natural ease."

I heard the most straightforward instructions for breath-awareness practice from Shirley, the radiation technologist doing my mammogram. I told her I was a meditation teacher.

"I believe in meditation," Shirley said. "I've been meditating for twenty years, religiously, every day."

"What do you do?" I asked.

"I pay attention to my breath," she said. "I get up every morning, wrap myself in a comforter, and sit on my couch for half an hour. I close my eyes and feel my breath come in and out. That's all. Sometimes I have trouble sleeping at night, but even if I do, that half hour in the morning refreshes me completely."

"You do that every day?" I asked.

"Oh yes," she replied. "Unless I get up too late, and my family is already up and making noise. Then I do yoga instead."

So much for fancy instructions.

Late Tea

I put late tea in the schedule because it's traditional at mindfulness meditation retreats. It's just tea. If you enjoy tea, prepare some now. Drink your tea slowly. Enjoy the smell of it. Feel the warmth of the cup in your hands. Take as long as you'd like. Even if you aren't having tea, use this time, as you would any other time, for cultivating calm, focused attention. Sit quietly. Try resting the attention in current experience. Be alert to the tendency of the mind to look ahead to what's happening next.

When you are eager to know what happens next, turn the page.

"Nothing Happens Next. This Is It!"

A few years ago a Gahan Wilson cartoon was making the rounds of bulletin boards in meditation centers. A seated figure, wearing what looks like a monk's robe, is whispering to the person next to him. He is saying, "*Nothing* happens next. This is it!"

I suppose the cartoon is meant to mildly mock meditation, perhaps suggesting that it is pointless. But I think the great truth of the cartoon is that "Nothing happens *next*." Now is the only thing that is ever happening. Now, when it is *clear*, is manageable.

On my desk, I have one of those round, fluid-filled globes with "snowflakes" in it that swirl up into a snowstorm when the globe is shaken and settle down at the bottom when the globe is still. When the "snow" stops falling, a lone snowman looks at me through the glass. During a "storm," I can hardly see him. I don't have an altar, and I don't *exactly* think of my globe as a religious icon, but if I did have an altar, I'd probably put my snowman in the middle.

Perhaps, someday, I'll put a little sign in front of the snowman that says, "Wait! Things will get clearer!" That would be a declaration of my faith—not complicated faith, not cosmological faith, but garden-variety, common-knowledge faith in the mind's tendency, like the snowman globe, to settle down if you leave it alone.

Settling down is what you were meant to do today. Tomorrow is a full day of formal mindfulness practice. Now is the time to go to bed.

PART THREE

Day Two

Full Day of Practice

Before Breakfast

Sound Meditation

One specific method for practicing mindfulness of body sensations is to focus your attention on sounds. Sounds, like everything else, arise and pass away. Just by listening, you can experience the insight of impermanence, an understanding the Buddha taught as crucial for the development of wisdom.

Early morning is great for listening. Sounds start to slip into the stillness. In a rural setting, the sounds are likely to be those of birds and animals waking up. In a city, sounds of outside action begin–garbage collection, building construction, traffic. Even in the rarefied air of a high-rise hotel room, plumbing sounds and elevator sounds and footsteps in the hall pick up in pace.

Sit in a position in which you can be relaxed and alert. Close your eyes. The stillness of your posture and the absence of visual stimuli both enhance hearing consciousness. People are sometimes surprised to discover how *much* sensory consciousness gets lost in the shuffle of distracted attention.

After your body is settled comfortably, just listen. Don't scan for sounds; wait for them. You might think of the difference between radar that goes out *looking* for something and a satellite dish with a wide range of pickup capacity that just sits in the backyard, waiting. Be a satellite dish. Stay turned on, but just wait.

At the beginning, you'll likely find that you are naming sounds: "door slam ... elevator ... footsteps ... bird ... airplane ..." Sometimes you'll name the feeling tone that accompanies the experience: "bird ... pleasant ... pneumatic drill ... unpleasant ... laughter ... pleasant ..." After a while, you may discover that the naming impulse relaxes. What remains is awareness of the presence or absence of sounds: "hearing ... not hearing ... sound arising ... sound passing away ... pleasant ... not pleasant."

Think of your listening meditation now as a wake-up exercise for your attention. However it happens—with names, without names, with feeling tone awareness or without—just let it happen. Don't try to accomplish anything. Just listen.

Breakfast

In our regular lives, we often eat breakfast *while* doing something else or *en route* to doing something else. This morning, just eat breakfast. Whenever we *just* sit, or *just* walk, or *just* eat, the mind calms down.

Be alert to the tendency of the mind to busy itself, looking around for things to watch or think about while eating. It's just a habit. Each time you notice it you lessen the tendency for it to happen again. The more attention you bring to the direct experience of eating, the more interesting it becomes.

Now, eat slowly, and savor the moment.

Three Exercises for Sitting Meditation

Exercise One

Basic instructions for mindfulness meditation usually tell you to begin by focusing on the phenomenon of breathing. We can practice mindfulness by paying calm, focused attention to anything, but we start with breath because it's convenient and regular. Thoughts, feelings, moods, and perceptions come and go. But breathing is always happening.

Breath is steadying. It is usually plain. Body sensations can be pleasant or unpleasant. Thoughts can be captivating, seducing the mind into stories. Breath, in its ordinariness, is calming. In addition, its rhythmically shifting pattern of arising and passing away is an ongoing presentation of the truth of impermanence.

You can pay attention to the breath in various parts of your body. You might want to begin by paying attention to the very small ways in which you can sense the breathing throughout your whole body as you sit quietly. Feel the subtle vibrations and echoes of each breath as it arises and passes away. Or you might feel the breath in the sensations of your belly moving in and out as your diaphragm pushes up and down. Perhaps you feel the sensations of the breath around the rib cage as you breathe in and out, and you might feel subtle pressures along the undersides of your arms. You may feel the sensations of the breath most prominently around the nostrils as subtle quiverings as the breath comes in and goes out. Sometimes, if the temperature outside is remarkably cooler than your body temperature, you can feel, as you exhale, that the breath has been warmed by your body. If you pay close attention, you may be able to feel the pressure of the breath on your upper lip as you exhale.

Sit for twenty minutes. Rest your attention wherever you feel the breath most clearly. Whenever you discover that your attention has wandered to something else, return it to the breath. Let everything else disappear into the background of your mind.

Question

My breath is the least interesting thing
happening. Can I make it interesting?
Can the rest really become background?

It can! Finding something special to notice about breath will allow the background action to disappear. I discovered the background-disappearing phenomenon before I discovered the Buddha. I discovered it at the ballet. During those years when my daughter Emily was dancing children's roles in *Nutcracker,* I imagined that I might be the mother with the record for attending the most performances. Probably I wasn't. Probably everyone else's mother had my same experience. Thirty or forty beautiful children would dance onto the stage, curtsey and bow through the minuet, "ooh" and "aah" at the tree, and applaud the dancing bear. Most of the time I saw only one person. Sometimes, perhaps if it was an evening performance and I had been to the matinee as well, my eyes let go of Emily and I noticed there were other things going on. But when she captivated my attention, everything else disappeared.

It wasn't just Emily's beauty that was captivating. Emily did look extraordinarily beautiful, with makeup, fancy hairdo, and shiny party dress. But so did all the other little girls. Also, I had the same experience when hers were one of eight pairs of legs in black tights sticking out under the Chinese dragon. Without knowing the lineup order, I knew which legs were hers, and hers were the ones I watched. They were just legs in black tights, but my interest made them extraordinary, and the background disappeared.

Exercise Two

Here is a way to make the breath more interesting to you, to help you keep it prominent in your experience. Sit again now, and notice that even in its regularity the breath goes through subtle changes.

The sensations that accompany the "in" breath are somewhat different from the sensations that accompany the "out" breath. As you relax and let the breath happen all by itself, you will be able to sharpen your attention by noticing how interesting and complex the simple act of breathing is. It's much more fascinating than you thought it was. You may notice that your breathing seems to slow down a little bit. That's normal. It may slow down because you are sitting still and because you probably are becoming a little bit calmer. Sometimes people worry that their breath will slow down *so* much or become *so* faint that it will disappear entirely. That never happens.

Close your eyes. Rest in the breath's regularity, and notice its constant, subtle changes. Sit for twenty minutes.

Question

You said the breath was always present,
but I'm starting to notice that there are
spaces between breaths.

I'm delighted that you've noticed. It probably means you've relaxed and you are paying attention. Breathing is a continuous function, but it's not continuously apparent. Breath comes in, breath goes out, and then there's a space. See if, as you sit, you can rest in that space. In classic texts, this space is called the "not-yet-arisen breath." Don't hurry to breathe the next breath in—the next breath will arise on its own whenever it's ready. There's a sense of ease that comes from letting the breath just happen. After a while, you may discover that not only is there a space between each whole breath, but there's also a space between the "in" breath and the "out" breath. As a matter of fact, the "in" breath doesn't *become* the "out" breath. The "in" breath, if you watch quite closely, is a separate and complete experience. It begins, it has a middle, and it ends. Then, there's a little space. After the space, the "out" breath arises anew, it has a zenith, and it entirely disappears. Now that you're starting to see the spaces, breath will become even more interesting.

Exercise Three

Rest in the arisen breath. Rest in the not-yet-arisen breath. Sit for twenty minutes.

Question

*I heard that people doing mindfulness
meditation are asked not to write in a
journal. Is that true?*

Yes, it is. Journals are wonderful, but while you are writing
in your journal, chronicling history, you are missing what
is happening now. Mindfulness meditation is a practice of
attending to now.

Debbie told the Wednesday morning meditation class
about her eighty-six-year-old mother who lives in a nurs-
ing home. The other residents spend time reminiscing
about their lives, especially about the extraordinary things
they have done. Debbie said, "My mother had a very full
life. She could tell lots of stories, but she doesn't. From
time to time she speaks up in a loud voice, stopping all
conversation: 'Listen,' she says, 'What was, *was!*'"

Question

*What if I have a wonderful idea?
Shouldn't I write that down?*

If it's really wonderful, you'll remember it.

Question

But what if it's a terrific idea?

If it's a terrific idea, write it down. But write briefly.

Talking to Yourself

In the Foundations of Mindfulness sermon, the Buddha's instructions for paying attention make it sound like meditators should go around talking to themselves. The sermon encourages meditators to notice "I breathe in a long breath," "I breathe out a long breath," "I am sitting," or "I am lying down." In the text, the recognition phrases are in quotation marks, and so sound like constant internal commentary.

Many mindfulness teachers suggest this specific technique of "mental noting" as a practice. Since I also find it helpful, I often recommend it. Mental noting *is* more or less constant commentary on present experience, but it has certain special characteristics.

First of all, it is not noisy. It's a quiet labeling of the current situation. The label "I am sitting," or even just "sitting," is a shorthand confirmation of "I am aware of a variety of body sensations that let me know I'm sitting. I *feel* myself sitting."

The second important characteristic of mental noting is that, although it is meant to be *continuous*, it doesn't need to be constant. It's not chatter. One mental notation of "I am sitting" could suffice, as long as the awareness rests calmly in the sensations of sitting. If the experience of mindful sitting should cause delight to fill the mind, one note of "I feel happy" or "rapture" is enough.

"Why should I tell myself what's happening?" students often ask. "Of *course* I know what's happening. It's happening to me, after all. I feel silly cataloging my experience. What good does it do?"

Mental noting, I tell them, has at least two benefits. It keeps the attention focused, and it offers moment-to-moment possibilities for the direct realization of temporality. Suppose my mental notations of my experience are "sitting . . . pressure . . . more pressure . . . tingling . . . rapture . . . happiness." Ongoing moments of awareness, cumulatively deepening composure, provide the context for the insight that experience is constantly changing.

Of course, these particular notes are just examples. The Buddha taught that paying attention in any situation—sitting, standing, lying down, moving—is the vehicle for developing understanding. What the particular notes *are* doesn't matter; that they change, *does.*

Continue your practice now, using the following instructions for formal walking meditation. Try mental noting as an aid in keeping the attention focused and alert. You don't need to name events exhaustively. That will make you more of a frantic list-maker than a composed meditator. I heard that the Buddha said there are 17 million mind moments in every experience. Forget about keeping up.

Basic Instructions for Formal Walking Meditation

Pick a place to walk back and forth that is private and uncomplicated—one where the walking path can be ten to twenty feet long. If you walk outdoors, find a secluded spot so that you won't feel self-conscious. If you walk indoors, find a furniture-free section of your room or an empty hallway. Then you can devote all your attention to the feelings in your feet as you walk.

Keep in mind that this is attentiveness practice and tranquillity practice, not specialty walking practice. You don't need to walk in any unusual way. No special balance is needed, no special gracefulness. This is just plain walking. Perhaps at a slower pace than normal, but otherwise, quite ordinary.

Begin your period of practice by standing still for a few moments at one end of your walking path. Close your eyes. Feel your whole body standing. Some people start by focusing their attention on the top of the head, then move their attention along the body through the head, shoulders, arms, torso, and legs, and end by feeling the sensations of the feet connecting with the earth. Allow your attention to rest on the sensations in the soles of the feet. This is likely to be the feeling of pressure on the feet and perhaps a sense of "soft" or "hard," depending on where you are standing.

Begin to walk forward. Keep your eyes open so that you stay balanced. I often begin with a normal strolling pace and expect that the limited scope of the walk, and its repetitious regularity, will naturally ease my body into a slower pace. Slowing down happens all by itself. I think it happens because the mind, with less stimuli to process, shifts into a lower gear. Probably the greed impulse, ever on the lookout for something novel to play with, surrenders when it realizes you're serious about not going anywhere.

When you walk at a strolling pace, the view is panoramic and descriptive. When your walking slows, the view is more localized and subjective. If we could see running readouts, like subtitles, of the mental notes that accompany walking, they might look like this:

Strolling pace: "Step . . . step . . . step . . . step . . . arms moving . . . head moving . . . smiling . . . looking . . . stopping . . . turning . . . bird chirping . . . stepping . . . stepping . . . wondering what time it is . . . thinking this is boring . . . stepping . . . stepping . . . swinging arms . . . feeling warm . . . feeling cool . . . I'm glad I'm in the shade . . .

deciding to stay in the shade . . . smiling . . . stepping . . ."

Slower pace: "Pressure on feet . . . pressure . . .
pressure disappearing . . . pressure reappearing
. . . pressure shifting . . . lightness . . . heaviness . . .
lightness . . . heaviness . . . lightness . . . Hey! Now
I've got it! Now I'm finally *present!* . . . Whoops,
I've been distracted . . . Start again . . . Pressure on
feet . . . pressure shifting . . . lightness . . . heaviness . . . lightness . . . heaviness . . . hearing . . .
warm . . . cool . . ."

Slow is not better than fast. It's just different. Everything changes, regardless of pace, and direct, firsthand experience of temporality can happen while you are strolling just as much as while you are stepping deliberately and slowly. The speed-limit guide for mindful walking is to select the speed at which you are most likely to maintain attention. Shift up or down as necessary.

Now, try a period of walking meditation. Start with thirty minutes. If you remembered to bring a timer with a pleasant "ding," set the timer and begin. If your watch has an alarm, you can use it as a timer. As you walk, note how many times the impulse to check the time arises. Don't do it. Just walk. This way, in addition to composure and attentiveness, you get to practice renunciation, a fundamental component of awakening.

Variation on the Theme of Breath Meditation

Sit down and feel your whole body sitting. You'll discover that you can tell where your body is without looking at it. Kinesthetic feedback from your body, myriad tiny sensations, let you know where your body is and what posture it's sitting in. You know if your legs are crossed; you know where your hands are. You don't need to look.

Feel your whole body. If you want to, let your attention move from the top of your head through your face, your neck, and your shoulders, down to your torso, now through your arms and your pelvis. Feel yourself sitting. You know that you are sitting because there's pressure on your bottom. Feel your thighs, your knees, your calves, your ankles, and your feet. See if you can hold the sense of your whole body in your attention at one time. Feel all of you, all of your body, in its seated posture. Here is your whole body sitting on the floor, sitting on a chair, sitting on the ground, sitting on your bed, sitting wherever it is sitting. Feel *all* of your body. It lets you know where it is with many, many sensations.

As you sit, those special events associated specifically with the coming and going of the breath are likely to become prominent. See if you can hold, simultaneously, the global awareness of all of the body sensations, as well as the particular awareness of the breath arising and passing away. This way, the body becomes the frame that is the context for the arising and passing away of the breath.

The regularity and predictability of the breath build composure in the mind. The wide-angle view of the shifting breath within the body provides an immediate example of the phenomenon of arising and passing away—the phenomenon that's true of all aspects of experience, an insight basic to this entire practice.

Close your eyes now. Feel your whole body, feel the breath arising and passing away within the context of the body, and, perhaps, to help the attention stay focused and composed with that experience, make the small notations in your mind: "breath arising, breath passing away; breath arising, breath passing away . . ." Try to sit for twenty minutes.

Question

I try to relax, and I try to focus on the
breath, but I can't stop thinking about a par-
ticular problem I am having in my life.
Maybe I should just try to figure it out, espe-
cially now that I have the time . . .

Often, people come to meditation retreats and decide, "Finally, I've got some free time–I'll figure everything out."
This usually doesn't work. If figuring worked, it would
have worked before the retreat. When solutions arise during meditation, they usually appear as revelations, not as
the result of figuring out.

Even without preplanning, the top ten of our psycho-
logical-emotional hit parade have a way of marching into
the mind whenever there is a break in the clouds. As soon as
space allows, the mind ruminates over memories or reflects
about the future–mostly with remorse or apprehension.

Suppose you rented a video, popped it into your
VCR, and sat down to watch. Suppose, ten minutes later,
you realized that you had already seen this video. Maybe
you had even seen it twice, renting it the second time because the cover seduced you. You would probably push
the eject button, set the video near the door so that you
wouldn't forget to return it, and read a book instead.

Suppose you rented a video and discovered after the
first ten minutes that not only were those first ten minutes

"Coming Attractions," but the whole tape was coming attractions. That would be boring and unsatisfying. You'd switch it off and do something else instead.

We forget that we have an eject button for mind stories. We ruminate and regret and reflect and rehearse endlessly. We probably pass by Now only briefly, on the way from Ruminating to Rehearsing, hardly pausing to relax. When we stop at Now, things become clear. We do what we need to do, or the best we *can* do, and move on. Stories of the past are history. Stories of the future are science fiction. Sometimes we need to plan, but not nearly as much as we think we do. Besides, plans have a way of changing.

Be aware, as you practice, of how stories begin to replay in the mind at odd moments, rather like capricious television sets that turn on at their own whim. Here you might be, sitting at ease, resting in the movements of the breath, or walking, feeling your feet, and suddenly, out of nowhere, comes the story of "My Failed Relationship" or "How Will I Ever Get out of This Job That Isn't Really Me?" You do need to know why the relationship failed so that you can avoid going through the same thing again, and if your job is wrong, and changeable, you need to plan. But not *now*.

Here's an instruction. If you see the story about to start, say to it, and to yourself, "Not now." Sometimes that's enough. You are not in denial—you'll attend to it sometime, but not now. Now, you are busy cultivating composure. Remind yourself that the composure itself might provide a new perspective from which a solution could spontaneously arise.

Sometimes a gentle rejection is not enough. The story stays. As a backup technique, I acknowledge the story, name and catalog it, and promise myself, "On the drive home I will think about this story for hours! But not now."

"Nothing Is Worth Thinking About"

My first five years of meditation practice were pleasant, albeit unremarkable. I liked going away on retreat. I liked sitting quietly. I liked the food. I enjoyed hearing stories about the Buddha. I *loved* the idea that it was possible to live peacefully, regardless of the particular circumstances of one's life.

Although I certainly passed the time at retreats following the schedule—sitting, walking, sitting, walking—my attention was all over the place. I believe, in retrospect, that I probably thought about *more* stories and *more* fantasies on retreat than off, just because I had more time to let the mind roam around. At home I had lots of tasks, busywork for the attention. On retreat, my mind was free to spin endless stories. And it did.

Then, one day, I was walking along a path, probably telling myself a story. My teacher Joseph Goldstein was coming toward me, engaged in conversation with another person. I didn't hear the whole conversation or even the sentence that preceded Joseph's remark. But just as they passed by me, I heard Joseph say, "Listen, nothing is worth thinking about."

"Nothing is worth *thinking* about?" I was stunned. I had spent my whole life thinking about everything. I come from a long line of heavy thinkers. I pride myself on my thinking. I also knew that Joseph was a pretty good thinker himself. How could he *say* that?

Somehow, by grace perhaps, or just because the necessary conditions had been met for me to "get" it, I "got" it. If the point of practice is to see in *this* moment, as in every moment, the truth of arising and passing away, the truth of eternal change, I need to be here, *now,* to see it. Stories are always mind-elaborations on the mythic past or the hypothetical future. They are not here.

So I took a vow not to tell myself stories. Not forever, but for the period of time I was on retreat, practicing. It wasn't a vow against all thinking, because cognitions—"moving, stepping, hungry, tired"—are thoughts, too. It was a vow about *discursive* thinking, which is what stories are.

As soon as I took the vow, my meditative experience changed dramatically. I determined that my attention, when I sat, would not wander away from the breath. The initial minutes of resolve, perhaps the initial hours of resolve, were difficult. Very soon, however, I found I *could* relax. It wasn't that I humbled the attention into submission. What happened was that the breath became interesting. In fact, fascinating. Even—can you believe it—thrilling! That's when my serious practice began.

Years later, I told Joseph about my transformation of understanding and transformation of practice. He said, "Maybe I didn't mean 'Nothing is worth *thinking* about.' Maybe I meant '*Nothing* is worth thinking about!'" But that's another story.

Now, sit for thirty minutes.

More Walking Instructions

In college I used a microscope with three levels of lens power. I would start with minimal magnification to scan the slide and shift to more refined levels to see individual items in detail. Sometimes specimens slipped out of viewing range just when I was seeing them in clearest focus. When that happened, I would back up and begin again.

Many years later, I adapted the microscope method for walking meditation. Here are the instructions. They are particularly suited to outdoor walking, where the breeze might be scented and the sun might be shining. If outdoors isn't an option, indoors will do.

Begin your walk with your *whole* body attentive to experience. Feel the temperature of the air on your skin. If there is a breeze, feel it press against you. Smell the air. Listen to the sounds around you. Imagine that your eyes are wide-angle camera lenses, and let them receive a panoramic view. Feel your whole body moving through space. Notice how, in ordinary walking, all parts of the body are naturally, unself-consciously involved. Your arms swing at your sides. Your hips move. Your balance shifts. No planning is needed for walking. Once you stand up with the intention to move, walking happens.

Walk back and forth on your walking path, feeling your walk with your whole body. After some time, perhaps ten minutes, shift your attention to the sensations in your legs. After a while, limit your attention to your feet. Perhaps you will then be able to focus clearly on the sensations in the bottoms of your feet: "pressure . . . no pressure . . . pressure . . . no pressure . . ."

Remain closely attentive to feet sensations as long as the focus is steady. At some point, it's likely your attention will begin to wander: "What's next?" "So what?" "I'm cold. I need a sweater." When this happens, back up your attention range. Feel your whole body walking. Feel the breeze, smell the air, listen. When your attention steadies, you can move in closer again. Moving the focus of awareness to adjust for levels of concentration will help you maintain composure. Staying alert is what counts. After all, we are becoming awareness experts, not walking experts.

My guess is that the microscopes I used in college are long gone now, probably valuable only as antiques. Specimens probably go in electron microscopes that automatically generate computer analyses. The microscope analogy still works for walking, though. Try it for the rest of this hour.

There Are No In-Between Times

Mindfulness meditation is continuous, calm, focused attention in all activities punctuated by periods of formal sitting and walking. The formal sitting and walking periods create the clarity that makes continuous practice possible. I finally understood this *years* after I began meditating, and my life became my practice.

I credit U Pandita, a Burmese meditation master, with providing this perspective. His style of interviewing was the clue. He would ask, "How mindful are you when you are sitting?" "How mindful are you when you are walking?" and "How mindful are you during in-between times?"

One day, as I prepared for my interview with U Pandita, I realized that even during retreats there is at least as much "in-between" time as formal practice time. Suddenly, activities that I had done casually, such as eating, showering, and making my bed, became valuable! Moving *between* activities became as important as the activities themselves. Instead of leaping up from my meditation cushion to hurry to my walking path, I let the journey itself become the practice. If I arrived at my path, walking slowly, just in time to return to my cushion, that was just fine.

I was delighted with my new understanding, because it meant I was *always* practicing and I never needed to do anything special. My life, I knew, would continue to unfold on its own as it always had. All I needed to do was *be* here.

So there are no in-between times. Preparing lunch, awaiting its arrival, and eating it are all times for mindfulness practice.

Introducing Eating
Instructions

Since we are getting ready to eat lunch, this is a good time to introduce the Second Domain of mindfulness, the second realm in which the Buddha taught we could pay attention. This is the realm of quality of feelings. The Buddha taught that one of three types of feelings–pleasant, unpleasant, and neutral–accompanies every moment of experience. It's true.

It is *not* the point of practice to make everything so bland that only neutral feelings are left. The point is to be alert to pleasant and unpleasant feelings, so that they don't frighten or sidetrack us as much as they normally would. Also, feeling tones are continually shifting. Just like physical sensations, they offer the possibility of noticing the phenomenon of change that permeates all experience.

Eating periods are the best time in a retreat, I think, to pay attention to the realm of pleasant and unpleasant feelings, because there is more promise of sensual excitement at mealtime than there is at any other time during the retreat. In fact, the anticipation of eating is exciting enough to wake up the faculty of alertness even before eating starts.

One of my personal routines at retreats is to make sure that I am last in line entering the dining hall. I can do an enormous amount of mindfulness practice standing in line. I can be aware of how I have already begun to salivate. I can be aware of the alarm that arises as I notice another meditator piling an enormous amount of food onto her plate. I begin to worry that there isn't going to be enough left for me. I can notice my disappointment as someone with a tray full of food passes by, and I discover that the principal ingredient of lunch seems to be celery. I choose the end of the line specifically, because I know my mindfulness in the moments of waiting will be heightened by the sensory excitement of smelling, looking, and salivating.

If you brought food along to prepare, watch the mind choosing. "Should I eat this now and that later?" "Did I bring enough?" "Why did I bring broccoli? I don't even like broccoli!" "I wish I had remembered the Tabasco sauce." Try not eating as you prepare. It requires some restraint, but it's good practice. Restraint builds composure in the mind. In your regular life, you might nibble as you cook. On retreat, conserve your alertness. Imagine you are standing last in line.

Different challenges arise if your food is being delivered. I went to a wonderful monastery last year with arrangements to do hermitage practice. This meant I was given my room, informed of the liturgy schedule, shown the room in which I would be served my solitary meals, and left alone. When I came to eat, I entered the room by an outside door. Inside, there was a small table set for one person. Across the room was a shelf with what looked like cupboard doors behind it. The doors opened from the other side, and the cook would pass food through, leaving it on the shelf. Sometimes when I arrived, the food was already there. On the second day of my practice, when I was still settling down and still getting used to being in strange surroundings, I sat down to a lunch of what looked like gray broth. It didn't smell very good. I tasted it, and it didn't taste very good, either. I had a terrible, fleeting thought that the cook, by mistake, had passed me a bowl of dishwater. I immediately corrected my thought and tried to convince myself that it was miso. Nevertheless, it neither looked good nor tasted good. Once I had thought my worrisome thought, the broth looked and tasted worse, and I was alarmed about eating it.

I looked around for ways to dispose of the soup without humiliating myself. If I left it in the bowl, I'd have to pass the bowl back full. There was no sink in the room. I looked around for a potted plant–there was no plant. I considered opening the door and tossing it out, but I was afraid I would be caught in the act. I decided that the only way to deal with the situation was to eat the soup. So I did. An hour passed, two hours passed–I felt fine. I realized the soup probably was miso or some variation of miso.

If someone is bringing your meals, watch the mind wondering. "When is she coming?" "What if she forgets to come?" "What if she brings broccoli?" "What if she brings too much food?" "What if she brings too little?" "What if she brings something I don't *like*?" The mind, in the altered atmosphere of retreats, can elaborate on simple liking and not liking to the point of high drama.

Eating Meditation

Eating is sensual, and fascinating, and *very* complex. The mind, when presented with pleasant stimuli, kicks into high gear. When your awareness is increased, eating can reveal fundamental truths about arising and passing away. Besides, it's fun.

Make the entire operation of eating part of the exercise. When your food has been prepared or delivered, experience it as fully as you can before you eat it. All the senses can be involved in eating. You can look at food, and smell it, and touch it. If it's crunchy, when you eat it you can even hear it!

If your food is attractive to you, you'll probably salivate, and the desire to eat it will arise. You may think, "Why am I sitting here *contemplating* this food? I want to eat it!"

Go ahead. Eat whenever you are ready. Eat slowly, though, because eating is complicated, and you want to learn all about it.

Pay as much attention as you can to chewing. Notice how the taste of food changes between the initial bite and the eventual swallow. Ranking beginning taste and final taste is irrelevant. The point is to notice change. Try to pay attention to what happens to the desire to eat. When you begin a meal, appetite is present. Sometime during the meal, appetite disappears. The liberating insight of the Buddha, "All conditioned things are transient," is as true of appetite as it is of anything else.

Feel free to enjoy your meal fully. Sometimes people imagine that meditation meals must be meager, minor events. I think the opposite is true. Since eating is such a whole-body, multi-sense event, use all of it for practice.

Maintaining
Mindfulness

Meditators often use the unscheduled time after lunch for resting, showering, or lying down. In terms of potential for developing insight, lying down counts the same as walking, brushing teeth, or eating—mindfulness is always the common denominator. What we are practicing is alert, composed awareness in *all* circumstances. Practicing on retreat is specialized preparation for practicing in regular life. It jump-starts the motor.

The technique of mental noting (naming experience as it unfolds) is *particularly* useful in maintaining continuity of mindfulness throughout an activity and during shifts in activities. It keeps the attention focused on present experience while you are showering or making a bed. Or while you're going from taking a shower to making the bed to sitting down to resting the attention in the breath.

People sometimes hesitate to use mental noting because it seems odd to them. It *is* odd, but it's very helpful. It tends to keep the mind clear and unconfused. Whatever you are doing now, keep track of your experience. Tracking starts out as a technique, but ends up as a habit.

In the early days of my practice, I felt tremendous resistance to doing mental noting, especially in the periods of going from one activity to another. My reluctance was based on a ridiculous piece of my personal history that was, at that time, about thirty years old.

When I was quite young, I had a boyfriend named Danny, who was probably as nervous about going out on dates as I was. I think he controlled his anxiety by talking to himself while, at the same time, keeping up a conversation with me. As we stood on a corner waiting for a bus and talking, under his breath he'd be saying, "Waiting for the bus, waiting for the bus, waiting for the bus, getting on the bus, taking out the money, paying the fare." I'm pretty sure poor Danny was doing it because he was nervous, and he was orienting himself in time and space. But I felt a little silly with him. I worried that someone I knew might see us. Or worse, they might hear him. How ironic that, thirty years later, I found myself doing a practice in which a major technique is labeling current experience. Mental notes like "reaching for the doorknob, touching the doorknob, turning the doorknob . . ." sounded to me like "waiting for the bus, waiting for the bus." I felt like an idiot. And every time I did it I remembered Danny. "I've gone mad," I thought. "Why am I doing this?"

Danny recollections aside, mental noting often seemed an extra burden. I would consider doing it and then decide, "Naah, this doesn't make sense." At some point or other, I took the instruction seriously and said to myself,

"Go for it–just do it. Don't think about it, don't evaluate it, don't figure it out, just *do* it."

When I did, everything changed. At first, I felt I was talking to myself: "Stepping, stepping, stepping, stepping, reaching, touching, turning, pulling." Then, suddenly, I was present to myself. My experience changed from lifting my arm and saying "lifting, lifting, lifting" to, all of a sudden, *knowing* lifting. I knew it in a different way than I had known it before.

Mental noting is not mindfulness. Mental noting is naming experience. Naming experience, bringing unwavering attention to experience, *leads* to mindfulness. Experiencing mindfulness *feels* different from talking about mindfulness.

A moment of mindfulness can feel ecstatic. I remember being amazed when I first began to discover the difference between talking about an experience and *being* the experience. The discovery of the rapture of mindfulness blew me away. Walking in a careful way, very present, I thought, "Talk about bizarre. *This* is bizarre: I'm totally thrilled about putting my foot down and *knowing* I'm putting my foot down." Putting a foot down is not normally the sort of thing we think of as thrilling. But it *is* thrilling. It's not the foot that is thrilling. Mindfulness is thrilling.

Afternoon
Sitting Practice

Wait and Look Closely

Here are instructions that will continue to refine your awareness.

Sit down. Relax. Feel your whole body sitting. Wait until you feel the breath happening. Don't pounce on it. Wait until it *presents* itself to you, until it arises in your awareness. Wait *attentively*, as if you expect it to arrive, so you are on the lookout for it. Wait with more or less the same relaxed vigilance that anticipates the regular, expected homecoming of a member of your household: genuine appreciation, no expectation of surprises.

Pay attention in a relaxed way; remain interested in your experience without getting caught. That's an important instruction. Interested is good. Caught is problematic. Being caught is being stuck, and being stuck in anything *isn't* being free.

Pay special attention in this sitting period to the arising of any moods or emotions that become distracting. If strong mind states arise, you can avoid being sidetracked by paying a little closer attention to the intricacies of each breath. There is a *lot* to notice about breath. Where do you feel it most clearly? In your belly? Rib cage? Around the nostrils?

What *exactly* do you feel? You don't *really* feel breath. In fact, there is no such *thing* as breath. Breath is the name we give to pressures and vibrations and shifts and changes of body sensations. How is an inhalation different from an exhalation? Can you experience them as separate phenomena? Are there beginnings? Endings? See? Not boring at all. Try it. Try to sit for forty-five minutes.

Working with Difficult Mind States

Perhaps, in this last period of sitting meditation, you became aware of the presence of particular states of mind, moods or emotions that were prominent enough for you to recognize. If they were pleasant, you probably enjoyed them. If they were unpleasant, you probably thought of them as difficulties and wished they would go away. Paying attention to mind states, and to their arising and passing away, is the Third Domain of mindfulness.

At this point it is helpful to address specifically the difficult mind states that characteristically arise in everyone's experience. Traditional texts list them as lust, aversion, sloth and torpor, restlessness, and doubt. Arcane as these may sound, they are commonplace. Read the following descriptions. Choose the one closest to your experience and follow the instructions for further practice.

Possibility I: You've thought of something wonderful you'd like to have and you cannot stop thinking about it. Perhaps you feel romantic, and you've spent the sitting period mentally composing a love letter. Maybe you are enjoying the retreat experience so much you are drafting and redrafting blueprints in your mind for a retreat cottage in your backyard. Turn to "Mine Mommy! Mine Daddy!" page 83.

Possibility II: You've become completely annoyed with this retreat situation. You are irritated about the retreat space, or the weather, or the instructions. You're annoyed with yourself for having decided to come. Turn to "Swimming in Jerusalem," page 87.

Possibility III: You are soooo-o-o sleepy. Lunch put you over the edge. Nothing seems more inviting than a long nap. Nothing seems remotely possible *except* a long nap. Turn to "Vait a Minute, Vait a Minute," page 91.

Possibility IV: You've thought of some problem in your life and are demoralizing yourself by worrying about it. "Phooey!!! I was having such a relaxed time. *Why* did I remember this now?" The problem is all you can think about. Turn to "Hawaii Is *Here*," page 93.

Possibility V: You've lost confidence in this whole business. The entire enterprise of sitting and walking, not *doing* anything, has begun to feel ridiculous. Or worse, worthless. This is a moment of doubt, disguised as legitimate opinion. Turn to "The Macbeth Moment," page 95.

Possibility VI: You are completely content, in which case you don't need special extra instructions. Now you could turn to "First Afternoon Walk Instructions," page 99.

Possibility VII: "Completely *content?!* I'm not content at *all!* I'm lonely, irritable, confused, and restless, and I don't for a minute believe there is any value to this!" You can take courage from the fact that even as you have these emotions, you've used up all the difficult mind states, and if you wait, things will settle down. Read straight ahead, all the way through to "First Afternoon Walk Instructions."

"Mine Mommy! Mine Daddy!"

A Lust Story

When people hear the Buddha's explanation "The cause of suffering is craving," they sometimes think that desire is a problem and that being spiritual means not desiring. That's not true. Desiring is a normal part of being alive. Getting stuck, single-pointedly, in a desire that *cannot* be met is what agitates and confuses the mind. It doesn't *cause* suffering. It *is* suffering.

My granddaughter Grace is two years old. She and I spent an evening together while her parents went to *The Phantom of the Opera*. Grace knows me well and had no problem with her parents leaving. She had waved, cheerfully, calling "Bye-bye, Mommy, Daddy."

We spent an hour reading *Sesame Street*, playing with her puzzles, watching her *Tubby the Tuba* video. Using "mind state" terminology, you might say that Grace and I both had balanced, alert minds, free of hindrance energies.

When I noticed her beginning to wilt, I said, "Let's get ready for bed, Grace." She was agreeable. We got her into pajamas, and, supplied with a new bottle of apple juice, the doll she sleeps with ("mine baby"), the doll's bottle ("mine baby bottle") and "baby's blanket," Grace climbed into bed, and I tucked her in.

"Bubbe, lie down, too."

"Okay, Grace, I'm lying down." Five seconds of silence.

"Mine mommy! Mine daddy!"

"Soon. Very soon."

"Mine mommy! Mine daddy!"

Grace had begun to lose her relaxed, balanced composure, and so had I. I glanced at the clock and calculated the time remaining before Sarah and Michael would return.

"Mine mommy! Mine daddy!"

"Soon. Here, I'll pat your back." I knew she likes to have her back patted gently, and I realized her little body was anxious because she was turning and wriggling, obviously *trying* to get comfortable.

"Pat back!"

"I *am* patting your back. Lie down. Close your eyes."

She flips over. "Pat stomach."

"I'm patting your stomach."

"Pat arm!" She sticks out her arm.

"I'm patting your arm."

"Pat *other* arm." She sticks out her other arm.

"I'm patting your other arm."

"Mine mommy! Mine daddy!"

"Soon!"

"Pat face."

"I'm patting your face."

It seemed to me that during the thirty-second interludes of patting–or the interludes when she became interested in her apple juice–her mommy-daddy-absent thought left her mind, and her body relaxed. "Whew," I would think, "now, if she could just accidentally fall asleep . . ."

Suddenly the thought was back. "Mine mommy! Mine daddy!"

Grace never totally lost it. She never even cried. But she clearly wrestled with the discomfort of her unmet need.

I didn't lose it, either, but I could feel my composure start to wobble. Just as Grace's tired mind had filled with the desire for mommy and daddy, *my* tired mind began to entertain thoughts of the casserole I had seen Sarah put in the fridge. The more time passed, the more I thought about the casserole. "When Grace falls asleep, I'll eat something . . . You just ate supper . . . How can you eat again? . . . It was just sushi . . . I'm hungry . . . The casserole is vegetables . . . I'll eat again."

"Mine mommy! Mine daddy!"

"Soon, Grace."

An hour later, Grace fell asleep. I could tell she was sleeping because her body relaxed, her eyes stayed closed, her breathing was regular, and she dropped her apple juice bottle. Already asleep, she whispered, "Mine mommy! Mine daddy!"

Grace dealt with her episode of uncomfortable desire by using restraint. She *didn't* cry. She (and I) thought of all the tools she could use to stay comfortable, and eventually her discomfort subsided enough for her to relax and sleep. I got up and ate some, but not all, of the casserole. I thought we'd both done well.

Meditation Instruction

Sensual feelings and fantasies come and go. They are the natural response of the mind to recognizing or recalling something pleasant. They need not be a problem. Acknowledging them reduces their power. Restrain the impulse to amplify a passing fancy into a full-scale mind drama by focusing your attention a bit more resolutely on the breath. Sit for another five minutes; bring all your attention to the breath. Resist the impulse to tell yourself stories. Then turn to "First Afternoon Walk Instructions," page 99.

Swimming
in Jerusalem

An Aversion Story

When unpleasant feelings fill the mind, the mind grumbles. It grumbles at anything in its path. It grumbles even if it knows better. I learned that lesson while swimming in Jerusalem.

The pool where I swim in Sonoma County, California, is very orderly. People swim back and forth; they know about lane lines and about swimming laps. When I arrive to swim, I can insinuate myself easily into any one of those lanes. I pick out a line of swimmers that seems to be moving at my speed and get in. Then we all swim in long circles, forward and back. People stay in line.

I spent a month in Jerusalem last year. As soon as I arrived, determined to continue to exercise, I joined the YMCA. The next day, after changing into my suit in the dressing room, I emerged, towel in hand, and saw the pool for the first time. It was full of very large women in shower caps, zigging and zagging in all different directions. I got in gingerly and attempted to swim back and forth. Almost immediately, I ran into somebody. She got mad. I apologized, but I don't speak Hebrew very well. She spoke to me in rapid-fire language I didn't understand. She called the attention of the lifeguard, pointing me out to him with angry gestures. I felt humiliated. I decided I would swim with my face out of the water so I could see where I was going and avoid hitting people. Even when people saw me coming, they didn't move. They had *conversations* in the middle of the pool!

I swam every day in Jerusalem, but I swam grimly, churning up irritable thoughts like "They should put in lane lines," "They should give protocol instructions," "If these women want to talk they should get out of the pool and talk." I swam back and forth fueled by righteous indignation. It wasn't pleasant. I wasn't happy.

One day after swimming, while changing in the dressing room, I relaxed my internal diatribe long enough to listen to the women talking to each other. They spoke a combination of Russian, Yiddish, and a little Hebrew—they were recent Russian immigrants. I looked at their faces and bodies—older, more tired, more worn out than mine. Lots of varicose veins. They had lived through fifty years of Soviet regime and through the war before that. I suddenly thought, "I am in a shower room full of naked Jewish women, and we are *safe*." I was very happy that they were alive and well and swimming in the pool at the Y and that I was there with them.

I was also very happy and *relieved* by my change of heart. "Whew," I thought, "now I'll be all finished with my irritable thoughts about these women, and I'll be able to swim peacefully in the pool with them." I told my husband my revelation. "Now I have my values straight," I said. "I love those women. They can swim however they want."

The next time I swam, the women zigged and zagged, and the irritable thoughts came back. When present circumstances are disappointing, aversion arises. That's just the way it is.

Near the end of my stay in Jerusalem, I told the YMCA story to a group of students to whom I was teaching meditation. I told it because I thought it would be a good, local illustration of how peace of mind is available only if we are prepared to let go of expectations that lead to recrimination. One of the students corrected me. "I think you did it wrong," he said. "You should have explained your situation to the lifeguard, and he would have taught the women to swim in lanes."

I think I must not have been teaching very clearly that evening. If I had been, my student would have understood that, even if the women had been swimming in lanes, the water was too warm. And the towels were too small. And too rough. As Gilda Radner very aptly put it in the title of her book, *There's Always Something*.

Meditation Instruction

Aversive feelings and fantasies come and go. They are the natural response of the mind to recognizing or recalling something unpleasant. They need not be a problem. Acknowledging them reduces their power. Aversive thoughts tend to build tension in the body, so stretch your arms and legs, loosen your shoulders. Try to smile. Sit for five minutes. Relax. Rest your attention on the sensations in your body. Then turn to "First Afternoon Walk Instructions," page 99.

"Vait a Minute, Vait a Minute"

A Sloth and Torpor Story

From time to time, the mind runs out of steam. Lacking energy, it feels confused, it daydreams, it falls asleep. Especially after lunch. Paying closer attention to every moment of experience—the Buddha called it "aiming the mind"—is, itself, the antidote to lack of clarity.

My friend Martha's ethnic roots are different from mine, and so she never had a grandfather who said, "Vait a minute," but she uses that phrase with me a lot. I use it often to signal lack of clarity. It's shorthand for "Let's slow down. Too much data is happening at one time. I am on overload. I am confused."

Focusing on one thing at a time cultivates clarity. Slowing down, doing less, makes it possible to aim the mind with precision.

My grandfather moved slowly, and he did one thing at a time. When he was very old, he came to live for a while in my home, and my children took him to school for show-and-tell. No one else had a ninety-five-year-old great-grandfather. He was a big help in our household. His health was wonderful, and he enjoyed chores.

His only limitation was his hearing loss, which was considerable. He needed to concentrate fully to understand what anyone was saying. That's where the "Vait a minute" password originated.

My grandfather might have been, for example, standing at the sink peeling potatoes. I would approach and begin talking. He would be concentrating on peeling, and besides, the water would be running. "Vait a minute! Vait a minute!" he would say. He would turn off the water, put down the paring knife, turn to face me fully, and say, "Now. Vhat?" *That* is aiming.

Meditation Instruction

Energy levels change in the mind just as they do in the body. Low energy states need not be a problem. Acknowledging them reduces their power. Sit for five minutes. Keep your eyes open. Try to aim the mind precisely by noticing the beginning and ending of each breath. Then turn to "First Afternoon Walk Instructions," page 99.

Hawaii Is *Here*

A Restlessness Story

In the middle of teaching a class for meditators called "Working with Difficult Mind Energies," I was reminded of how the nearest oasis is always right under our feet. The topic for the evening was Restlessness, the tendency of the overly energetic mind to scan the environment for possible sources of worry and spin them into frets. Having spent a lot of my life as a high-level fretter, and being now substantially recovered, I teach these classes with particular enthusiasm. I'm positive my recovery is a result of my meditation practice, so I am eager to spread the word.

Nancy, one of the newer students, said, "It's a curious thing. When I am around home, I can hardly let go of my obsessive worrying. If it's not one thing, it's another. But the mind seems to have a geographical statute of limitations. All my fears fall away if I go to Hawaii."

"Hawaii is *here*!" I responded immediately. "It really *is*. Look! No palm trees, no beaches, but the Hawaii solution, which could also be the Toronto solution, is a reflection of the mind's awareness that I can't *do* anything about that situation right now."

Every moment of mindfulness, every moment of re-laxed, alert presence, every moment in which the mind is not grasping at something it thinks it needs or trying to get away from something it thinks it doesn't want is a moment of freedom. Sometimes it's called "presence," which has a special, lofty sound about it. I think it's simpler than that. When we are present, we see what needs to be done. We also see the limits of what we can do. Everything *else* is out of our hands. What a relief!

Meditation Instruction

Energy storms come and go in the mind, whipping up fidgets and alarm. They need not be a problem. Acknowledging them reduces their power. Breathe some long, slow, deliberate breaths. Relaxed breathing calms the body and settles the mind. Sit for five more minutes, attending to easy breathing. Then turn to "First Afternoon Walk Instructions," page 99.

The Macbeth Moment

A Doubt Story

One particular meditation event happened to me with such regularity that I came to think of it as inevitable. I recognize it now as an experience of almost-insight in a mind confused by some boredom and maybe some grumpiness. At the time, my response was, "Uh-oh! Here it goes again." I didn't like it.

I would be walking along, practicing as diligently as I could. Suddenly, as if someone had popped a tape player into my mind, I would hear, "Tomorrow, and tomorrow, and tomorrow, / Creeps in this petty pace . . . / And all our yesterdays have lighted fools / The way to dusty death . . ." Macbeth, once again, alerting me to the fact that my experience has become tedious.

The Macbeth Moment always stretched into continuous repetitions once it began. Starting with "Tomorrow . . ." it would roll all the way to "It is a tale, / Told by an idiot, full of sound and fury, / Signifying nothing" and then start over again. I pictured a cosmic, invisible actor rehearsing his lines directly into my mind. When my situation reminded me of a tape recorder set on auto replay, I tried, using mental imagery power, to eject the tape. It rarely worked.

"Why am I *here*?" I would think. "This is all futile. Sunrise, sunset, endless cycles passing inexorably by, and all of us self-consciously doing 'spiritual practice to become enlightened' and who knows what *that* means anyway?" I would feel melancholy about *my* plight and everyone else's plight, and then I'd feel depressed about my despair. "It's all a hoax!" I would think. "And somehow we've all believed it—and here we are in ridiculous, empty pursuit."

The Macbeth Moment is, I believe, a skewed interpretation of some crucial truths. Tomorrow *does* keep arriving, at its own regular pace, making us and all our experiences and possessions quite perishable. We can neither hold on to nor fend off the passage of time. And although "a tale told by an idiot" seems an irreverent way to recognize the fact that cosmic design unfolds in dimensions far too huge for individuals—certainly for me—to comprehend, it is a dramatic reminder of the fragility and unpredictability of life. Events often seem arbitrary.

The Buddha taught that nothing happens without an antecedent cause, and nothing happens without generating some effect. From this perspective, the cosmos is lawful. (When I first heard my teacher Joseph say, "It's a lawful cosmos," I thought he was saying "It's an awful cosmos," and I agreed!) The liberating potential of this understanding is that it brings freedom from taking everything personally. It means doing the best we can to take care of everything—ourselves, all beings, the planet—and also re-membering that we are not in charge.

One of the insights that people practicing mindful-ness meditation hope to achieve is the awareness of inter-relatedness. The Macbeth Moment is not a mistake. It's dramatic (because that's my style) and somewhat dreary ("creeps" and "petty" are not celebratory words), but it does tell the truth about the ultimately empty nature of time and experience. "Full of sound and fury, / Signifying nothing" is a great description of what all the carryings-on here would look like from a cosmic vantage point.

Eventually, all my Macbeth Moments have settled down into some greater appreciation of what seems to be just plain truth. Time does pass. Things do happen. Who knows why? We somehow manage. The shift in my own experience from agitated gloom to relaxed acceptance happens, I think, when I start to laugh. I think it comes with the nth replay of the soliloquy when I get to the words "That struts and frets his hour upon the stage / And then is heard no more." I look at the other meditators around me and think, "Look at us all strutting and fret-ting!"

Meditation Instruction

It's normal to feel moments of doubt in which the atten-tion stumbles and resolve weakens. Everyone has these moments. They need not be a problem. Acknowledging them reduces their power. Stay alert for sabotaging thoughts: "You're doing it wrong," "This is too hard." You're doing it right, and it's easier than you think. Sit for another five minutes. Sustain your attention on each breath, from beginning to end. Then turn to "First Afternoon Walk Instructions," page 99.

First Afternoon
Walk Instructions

Choosing a Speed That Meets Your Need

Concentration does not develop because you stick to a particular walking speed. It develops because your attention stays focused on the activity. If you walk very slowly but your mind is all over the place thinking ten thousand different stories in between each step, you could walk to the moon without building concentration. If you run around the block ten times and you pay attention to each footstep as it touches the ground, you would be quite focused and concentrated by the end of the run. The key factor in developing concentration is keeping the forward motion at a speed at which your attention can stay focused.

Awareness of the transience of experience can also develop at any speed. If you walk very slowly, paying close attention, you will notice, with each step, that the pressure on the bottom of the foot decreases until it has vanished and then reappears. Your experience will be the arising and passing away of minute sensations of pressure, tingling, and heaviness under the feet.

If you run around the block paying close attention, you will notice, instead of minute foot sensations, scenes appearing and disappearing. As you run down one street, a particular view is present. As you turn the corner, suddenly there's a *new* view. You discover arising and passing away in a much more macro way than you would while walking slowly. It doesn't matter if waking up is macro or micro—it only matters that it happens.

It's important not to have a goal of *getting* somewhere when you walk. If you want to walk slowly, walk back and forth on your short walking path. If you want to move quickly, pick a longer route. Just don't *go* anywhere. Practice for forty-five minutes.

Late Afternoon
Sitting Practice

Looking for Insights

The experience of insight about how things are—realizing the truth about suffering, understanding the energies that confuse the mind, perceiving the factors that lead to enlightenment—these are what the Buddha called the realm of the dharma, the Fourth Domain of mindfulness. Insights, like everything else, arise and pass away. Repeated insight leads to wisdom.

You cannot just sit down and say, "Now I'm going to practice understanding, insight, and wisdom." They happen by themselves. They are the fruits of practice.

You've been awakening awareness using specific instructions for sitting, walking, and eating. All the instructions are variations on the theme of deconditioning the mind from its habitual patterns. Following instructions requires effort. You tried to let your attention rest exclusively on the breath. You tried to feel sensations in the body as you walked. You tried to be attentive to liking and not liking, and you tried to work with difficult mind states. All the trying was in the service of calming down the mind and helping it focus. Now, don't try.

The instructions for this sitting are: don't just do something, sit there. Sit with your eyes open or closed. Relax. Be expectant, without anticipating. Breath comes and goes, body sensations come and go, sounds come and go. Feeling tones and mind states come and go. Everything comes and goes, all by itself.

If, as you sit, your attention gets *caught* in particular events—thoughts or moods or feelings—you'll have a direct experience of the cause of suffering. It won't matter if these events are pleasant or unpleasant. The mind caught in clinging *or* aversion is uncomfortable. It's not free.

If, as you sit, your attention does *not* get caught in particular events, you'll have a direct experience of the end of suffering. Pleasant or unpleasant will not matter. You will be able to notice, with relaxed interest, the passing show of all phenomena. The alert mind, unruffled by clinging or aversion, is comfortable. It is free.

Late Afternoon Walk

Walking with Wisdom

Mindfulness meditation doesn't change life. Life remains as fragile and unpredictable as ever. Meditation changes the heart's capacity to accept life as it is. It teaches the heart to be more accommodating, not by beating it into submission, but by making it clear that accommodation is a gratifying choice. Accommodation of the heart is not always easy. Knowing that it is a possibility is a great inspiration. Having an accommodating heart is the ultimate freedom.

Practicing accommodation on the small, moment-to-moment disappointments of life—not *forgetting* our preferences, but remaining spacious and relaxed when preferences are not met—prepares us to deal with the larger challenges of life. The movement of the heart in surrender, in graceful accommodation, is bigger and more difficult when faced with the great griefs of life than with the minor inconveniences. Mindfulness meditation is a way of practicing that movement, using the plain business of our everyday lives as grist for the mill.

Take a walk in a leisurely, looking-around way. Notice, if you can, the way in which even one day of quiet mindfulness cultivates a more relaxed mind. The accommodating capacity of the mind, described in the texts as malleability, is a sign of wisdom. I imagine the mind looking around and saying, "Hey, this is it. Like it or not, this is what's going on."

The Broccoli
Phenomenon

The Broccoli Phenomenon, a classic illustration of the malleability of the mind, is reported to me regularly on retreats. Probably plenty of people who attend mindfulness retreats aren't crazy about broccoli. You might be one of them. The soup served for supper on the first evening is full of broccoli bits. "Hmm," you might think, "I'm not sure I'll be happy here. I hope this is the last of the broccoli." You begin to practice mindfulness, sitting still for certain periods, walking slowly for other periods, feeling your breath as you sit or your feet as you walk.

You begin to calm down. Breakfast is no problem. No scrambled eggs, no sweet rolls, nothing very interesting, but nevertheless okay. Then lunch. A huge stew appears, full of assorted vegetables, *including* broccoli. And steamed rice. "Uh-oh. How should I do this? Should I just eat rice? No, I'll be hungry. I guess I'll put the stew over the rice and pick *out* the broccoli. I hope they don't do this to me again!"

They do. The mind devotes an inordinate amount of air time to the dreaded broccoli:

"*Where* do they get these cooks?"

"When I get home, I'm sending them a collection of *good* cookbooks!"

"What if a person were *allergic* to broccoli?"

"Maybe I should leave a note for the cooks. They have no *idea* . . ."

"I bet if I saw their shopping list, *broccoli* would be the main item!"

"If they are *determined* to serve so much broccoli, they could at least cook it separately, as a side dish, and not mix it into everything else."

Days pass, meals pass, and between bouts of culinary criticism that temporarily cause mind storms, you continue to develop composure. Sitting, walking, breathing, stepping—hour by hour, gradually, while you are busy concentrating, your mind smoothes itself out. It happens steadily, but usually unremarkably, so sometimes you don't realize it's happening.

The Broccoli Phenomenon is how you can tell the practice is working. You enter the dining hall, broccoli is again prominently featured, and you experience nothing much in the way of a reaction. The mind accommodates. Maybe you even smile. Maybe you even have the thought, "Now I hope they don't leave out the broccoli at any meal because, if they do, I won't have nearly as good a story to tell when I get home."

If mindfulness meditation worked only with broccoli, it wouldn't be as valuable as it is. Mindfulness meditation addresses the broccolis of life, the inevitable pains of the body and disappointments of mind that are continually and fundamentally our experience.

The point of practice is not to be finished with pain forever, because we can't be. Nor is it to get over being pleased and then being displeased, liking and not liking, because these are natural responses to life. Mindfulness practice smoothes out the mind so that it sees clearly and responds wisely.

I seem to myself wiser on some days than I do on other days. My level of wisdom is more a reflection of my degree of mindfulness than of external life circumstances. The mind, when it is relaxed, makes sounder judgment calls.

Shanti, the head cook on many of the meditation re-treats at which I teach, told me the advice she got from Mrs. Hammond, her third grade teacher, about overcom-ing aversion to arithmetic. "Listen," Mrs. Hammond said, "You are going to have to do some sort of arithmetic every day for the rest of your life. You might as well enjoy it!"

Joining the ranks of Mrs. Hammond, I add, "We are going to experience some sort of broccoli every day for the rest of our lives." Some will be trivial, minor unpleas-antnesses, and some will be very, very hard.

Shanti doesn't use too much broccoli in her cooking. Even if she did, that wouldn't be a problem for me. I rather like broccoli. It's celery that's my problem.

Dinner

Here are more eating instructions. You already know the technical instructions: look at the food, smell it, savor it, and eat slowly. Lunchtime instructions included paying attention to feeling tone responses to food (pleasant . . . neutral . . . unpleasant), as well as awareness of the pursuant mind states (Yum! . . . Hmmm . . . Yuck!). This evening meal can include attention to the encompassing Fourth Domain of mindfulness: awareness of the truth of experience.

Read these instructions first, and then follow them. Sit in front of your food for some minutes before you eat. Notice what *exactly* happens to cause eating to start when it does. It's a voluntary action, so something has to happen. What is it? What happens just before that moment? What happens just after? Notice that you chew for a while, and then you swallow. What determines the swallowing moment? Is it a thought? A body sensation? How does swallowing happen?

What determines when you pick up the next forkful (or spoonful) of food? Picking up is a voluntary action, so *something* happens. What is it? What happens in your mind if you interrupt some food en route to your mouth and put it back on the plate? (Don't do this last exercise more than once—you'll annoy yourself!)

Can you notice the precise moment in which your appetite disappears? Where did it go? Are you disappointed? Notice if your food disappears before your appetite disappears. Are you disappointed?

This is a *general* outline. If you bring an investigative, alert approach to eating, there is as much truth to learn over dinner as anywhere else.

You might think of this as very self-conscious eating, but Buddhists don't believe in a self. Think of it as conscious eating.

Evening Dharma Talk

The Seven Factors of Enlightenment

The teaching style of the Buddha, twenty-five hundred years ago, was didactic. He gave talks. He walked all over India for forty years, and wherever he went, people gathered to hear him. Often they became enlightened just by listening.

A lecture in the style of the Buddha explaining a philosophic view or a meditative technique is called a "dharma talk." These talks have become traditional at contemporary mindfulness meditation retreats. Students look forward to them. Like the meals, they are a major stimulus hit in an otherwise sparse schedule.

When I began teaching meditation, I was surprised to find I was hesitant about giving a talk; I was not my usual confident teaching self. Teaching Buddhist philosophy felt different from teaching developmental psychology or, for that matter, anything else I had previously taught. Secular, scientific subjects had linked me horizontally with other contemporary teachers. Teaching meditation suddenly linked me through all the generations to the Buddha. I felt awed—after all, people became *enlightened* listening to the Buddha—and honored.

I relaxed about teaching as meditation became less mysterious to me. It *is* a science. Also, teaching about the Buddha involves telling lots of stories, and I am a storyteller. Over the years, listening to my teachers, I heard them give the same talks and tell the same stories over and over again. Because all the talks and all the stories convey the same message—peace is possible, in this very life and in this very body—I never got tired of listening to them.

My favorite talk was The Seven Factors of Enlightenment, the explanation of the special mind capacities of enlightened people. When I first heard that wise people radiated these seven qualities naturally, and in perfect balance, I thought, "Too hard! That doesn't sound like me at all!" When I heard I could *cultivate* these qualities, practice them in advance of them manifesting spontaneously, I felt better.

What follows is an interactive dharma talk on cultivating the factors of enlightenment. Read on, read each section, and pause whenever you arrive at practice instructions so that you can experience the seven factors personally.

None of the factors of enlightenment are capacities outside the range of normal human experience. They are commonplace. Concentration, calm, and equanimity are nuanced variations of composure. Rapture, energy, and investigation are the active ingredients of alertness. Mindfulness, the nonreactive, full understanding of present experience, appears in traditional lists as both the seventh factor of enlightenment and the sum of the other six factors.

Everyone has had experiences of deep concentration. They happen naturally whenever the attention is totally captivated. Awareness becomes single-pointed in focus, and time perception is altered. It happens to musicians, especially in ensemble groups. It happens to skiers and mountain bikers on steep trails. It happens to readers of spy stories who start a Ludlum novel during take-off in Boston and are surprised, six hours later, to be landing in San Francisco. Think of times when you are naturally concentrated. Recall how concentration feels.

Now, try to concentrate *only* on your breath. After you read these instructions, put down the book and close your eyes. Allow the breath to present itself to you wherever it appears most prominently. Keep your attention focused. Resist *any* impulse for the attention to wander. It requires some effort; it's not totally relaxed practice. But it's worth it. It builds concentration. Use a timer, if you have one. Sit for ten minutes.

Rapture, in meditation language, is heightened awareness of body sensations. It happens spontaneously when the attention is focused. I've felt my body pushing and breathing as I watched swimmers racing, or women in labor, or people about to die. When attention is focused and alert, awareness of body energy is enhanced.

Rapture arises in meditation as well. Some rapture experiences are strong enough to be visible to other meditators at retreats, who then may start to worry: "Uh-oh! I wonder why that person is rocking from side to side. I hope that doesn't happen to me!" or "What is that person smiling about?" or "Why is that person crying?" or "Why *isn't* that happening to me?"

Rapture arises in many forms and not all of them happen to everyone. Usually, meditation rapture is mild. As the mind and body quiet down, the body relaxes. People report feeling pleasantly warm or delightfully cool or generally tingly or amazingly light and spacious. Sometimes it's as simple as goose pimples.

Feel the rapture in your body right now. Sit relaxed and very still. Feel your whole body. Notice its energy. Is it tingly? Vibrating? Pulsing? Is it warm? Cool? Heavy? Light? Bring all your attention to some particular part of your body, such as your left elbow or your right ankle. Notice that when you do, that area responds with an apparent increase of sensations. It wakes up in your mind. Do that sequentially now, starting from your feet and moving through your body to the top of your head. Wake up your whole body with consciousness. Do it now. Sit for ten minutes.

Calm is a sense of smoothness in the mind. Tranquillity is often used as a synonym for calm. Unrufflable or unflappable would also work.

Dipa Ma, an elderly Indian woman renowned as a meditation teacher, visited the United States fifteen years ago. My teachers were her students, and they were eager to introduce her to other students in the mindfulness community. Classes were scheduled in my living room because it was large enough for many people to attend.

Dipa Ma was a very small woman, and at the time of her visit, my household included a very large akita. Akitas are formidable looking dogs, and normally guests hesitated before entering and needed reassurance. Dipa Ma sailed right on in. Yuki rose to greet her. They were almost equal size. She was taller; he was heavier. She put her hands on his head and blessed him. She had tranquillity. It was her long suit.

My favorite tranquillity story comes from my friend Anna, a teaching colleague at Spirit Rock Meditation Center. Long ago, during a period in which she was doing intensive meditation practice, Anna discovered a "completely new mind state." She describes being aware of its newness and its unfamiliarity, and says, "For a while, I wondered what it was. Then I realized it was calm."

Usually when Anna describes that experience people laugh. I think the laughing is only partly caused by her witty way of telling the story. The rest, I think, comes from ruefulness. People realize they rarely feel calm.

Practice the feeling of calm. Sit still, but be sure your body is relaxed. In a moment you'll close your eyes. When you do, allow your attention to rest on your breath, using the regularity of the movements of the breath to cultivate calm. There is a line in the Foundations of Mindfulness Sutta in which the Buddha says, "The practitioner can reflect taking a long breath in, 'I calm my body,' letting a long breath out, 'I calm my body.'" You can do the same. Try it now. Sit for ten minutes.

Investigation is that quality of mind which meets experience with the expectation that deeper looking will reveal hidden secrets. It requires some faith. Someone recently gave me a book of stereograms, drawings that initially appear as random, flat designs, but that jump out into a three-dimensional image when viewed correctly. I look and I look and I look. I pull the book up close to my nose, and move it away slowly, just as the instructions advise, and usually, nothing happens. I keep on trying. I have faith, because my husband says, "Look! Look! It's right there! Just cross your eyes. Just relax." I know the "truth" of the pictures is visible, because he sees it, and also, in *some* of the pictures, I see it. So I keep trying to look at each picture *as if* this time I'll see. I keep investigating.

Sometimes I approach a meditation session as if it were about to reveal a deeper understanding. I say to myself, "May I understand more fully about impermanence during this sitting," or "May I finally get it about interconnectedness." Sometimes I realize something new. Sometimes I don't. Every investigation doesn't yield new data, but investigating is necessary if anything is to be found.

Read these instructions for cultivating the quality of investigation, and then practice. Investigate beginnings and endings. Notice how every experience, long or short, begins and ends. You can begin with breath: "Breath begins, breath ends." You can also notice beginnings and endings of other body sensations: "Itching happening, itching gone." "Tingling beginning, tingling ending." Notice how thoughts begin and end, passing by like the flashing light news headlines in New York City's Times Square.

If, after a while, you are inclined to investigate further, you might look closely at where the breath, or the body sensations, or the thoughts, came from. Or where they went. Or who owned them. What noticed them? This quality of investigation is not a mandate to *figure it out*, but an openness to insight should it be ready to arise. Now, sit for ten minutes.

Equanimity doesn't mean keeping things even; it is the capacity to return to balance in the midst of an alert, responsive life. I don't want to be constantly calm. The cultural context I grew up in and the relational life I live in both call for passionate, engaged response. I laugh and I cry and I'm glad that I do. What I value is the capacity to be balanced between times.

One of the first meditation research papers I read, probably in the early 1970s, described a study designed to test distractibility. It also tested startle response. Meditators doing a practice of calm vigilance, such as mindfulness, were wired up to EEG machines that recorded their brain wave patterns. As they sat in meditation and produced the expected alpha waves, researchers rang bells or buzzers at random moments. The meditators' EEG patterns registered startle responses, but they very quickly resumed the relaxed wave patterns of calm, focused attention.

Imagine that you are one of the landmark research subjects. Put this book down. Close your eyes. Stay alert. Watch the mind respond to stimuli—sounds outside, thoughts and feelings inside—and see how *noticing* them restores the mind's balance. It *does* do it. Try it and see. Sit for ten minutes.

I saved the factor of energy for next-to-last mention because it becomes more evident as the other factors develop. Energy is sometimes defined as interest. I think of it as enthusiasm for practice. Zeal is a great word for it.

Energy is the response of the mind to the possibility that practice works. "Hey! Look at this! I *am* able to concentrate. I *am* calm. I *get it* about equanimity. I even *feel* a little rapture. I bet I really *can* do this."

My personal practice zeal level shot up incrementally after I vowed to stop telling myself stories and start paying attention to current experience. Initially I struggled, because I find my stories interesting. Very soon, however, the rapture that accompanies concentration became more interesting than my stories. Comedians in the early days of television often started routines with "Stop me if you've heard this one before . . ." My stories self-destructed; I'd heard them all before.

I began to love to practice. The joy of being present and the delight of discovering how the mind and body work were stunning surprises. I began to understand what my teachers had meant by the term *effortless effort*.

Sit for a while now. Perhaps my own zeal inspired you, and you feel energy for practice. See if you can practice, energetically, combinations of mind qualities. Concentrate on the breath, and then use the factor of investigation to see something new. *Expect* to learn something. As you concentrate, seeing deeply, feel your whole body. Enjoy its vibrancy. Practice smiling. It makes a difference.

Mindfulness is the seventh factor of enlightenment. I imagine how a chemist would write the equation for mindfulness: concentration + calm + equanimity + rapture + energy + investigation = mindfulness. Or, mindfulness equals the balanced, alert recognition of present experience.

In life, all the factors don't stay present in equal amounts all the time. We are more calm or less calm, more interested or less interested. That's normal. Energy shifts in the mind and the body, and circumstances change.

Practicing mindfulness in every moment, greeting each experience with alert, composed awareness, balances the other six factors. Cultivating each of the other six factors individually builds the capacity for mindfulness. Isn't that neat? I love it! You can't do it wrong.

Sit for as long as you like now. Enjoy yourself. Greet each moment with alert, composed awareness.

Evening Walking Instructions

You have practiced being mindful in all four realms that the Buddha outlined in the Foundation of Mindfulness sermon. You paid attention to body sensations, to feeling tones, to mind states, and to insights. The Buddha taught them separately, but he didn't teach that they are mutually exclusive. They aren't separate. They couldn't be–nothing is. You can practice all four perspectives together.

Every moment of awareness can be described in terms of the body sensations that are present. In walking practice, body sensations normally predominate. In sitting practice, physical sensations may be so subtle that the body seems to disappear. Either way, the experience can be named.

Every moment of awareness can also be characterized by its mind state. Sometimes new students think "mind states" mean *strong* emotions. They say, "I didn't have any mind states today." Strong emotions are easily perceived. Awareness of subtle mind states requires nuanced attention.

Every moment of awareness is accompanied by a feeling tone. We tend to notice pleasant and unpleasant moments more than neutral ones, because they attract or alarm us. In neutral moments, we lose interest. We space out.

Every moment of awareness also offers the possibility of realizing truth.

For this walking period, use all four perspectives for viewing experience.

In the first minutes of your walk, allow your attention to rest in your body sensations. Feel your whole body, feel your feet. As you continue to walk, begin to notice the predominant feeling tone of your experience: pleasant, unpleasant, or neutral. By and by, begin to ask yourself, "What mind state is present now?" From time to time, say to yourself, "What is true?"

You can change the four lenses as frequently as every breath, every five minutes, or whenever you feel like it. There's only one truth.

Looking from all perspectives, simultaneously, gives us the best view. It's something like a Picasso painting in which you see all the sides and the overhead view at the same time.

Last Evening Sitting

One Scribble Away from Enlightenment

Here are special instructions for practicing sitting meditation at times when you might be feeling sleepy.

The Buddha said we ought to be alert enough to know whether we wake up on an "in" breath or on an "out" breath. I don't think he meant only when we wake up in the morning. Waking up from a daydream is the same as waking up from sleep.

We wake up hundreds of times a day. Realizing we've been daydreaming–"Hey! Where was I?"–is a moment of alert awareness. Noticing, in that moment, whether the breath is on its way in or on its way out is a natural way of maintaining the energy of mindfulness.

Skip all the possible self-recriminations: "What a bad meditator I am!" "I'll never get the hang of this!" "I bet I'll spend the whole retreat asleep!" Doubting thoughts fatigue the mind. Use the energy of the moment of alertness to fully appreciate current experience: "I'm breathing in." Or "I'm breathing out." Or "I'm awake!"

I learned about using the energy of mindfulness from U Sivali, a Sri Lankan monk who was teaching at a retreat at which I was a student many years ago. I had described to him my dismay over a particular practice hurdle I was experiencing at retreats. It was my habit, in those days, to go to bed quite early, around nine o'clock at night. I would awaken refreshed in the middle of the night, get dressed, and go to the meditation hall to practice sitting and walking. I would arrive filled with enthusiasm, and five minutes after I started sitting, I'd begin to doze off. The rest of the night was sitting–dozing–walking–dozing–sitting–dozing. "Perhaps," I said to him, "this doesn't count for anything, and I should stay in bed."

"No," he replied. "Don't stay in bed. First of all, the intention counts. More than that, it doesn't matter how many times you doze off. What matters is that from time to time you wake up. Every moment of mindfulness erases a moment of conditioning!"

That last line, the idea that every moment of mindfulness *erases*, was an enormous boost to my capacity for patience. I imagined that my mind was a great scribbled-up blackboard, and in every moment that I paid attention, I was erasing scribbles. I thought to myself, "We never *know* how near we might be to erasing the last scribble! I might be one scribble away from enlightenment!"

Put this manual down now and try your sitting practice again. Try to be attentive to the breath every time you wake up. Whenever you have the thought "Where *was* I?" substitute "Where *am* I?"

However You're Doing, You're Doing *Really* Well

Here's a method I learned from my friend Jack for evaluating your meditation retreat performance while it's happening.

Jack established this criterion many years ago when a retreat manager asked him, as the teacher, about a particular student. Jack replied, "He is doing *really* well." The manager then asked about someone else, a person she knew had been having a rough time. Jack thought a while before responding, "She's doing really well, too." The manager, beginning to sense that the answers formed a pattern, asked about yet another person. "Oh yes," Jack replied, "he's also doing really well."

"What exactly do you mean, Jack, when you say people are doing really well?"

"I mean," he answered, "that they're still here."

You're doing *really* well, too.

End of
Day Two

If you're able to have a longer retreat, repeat the schedule for Day Two. Day Two is the prototype for a full day of mindfulness retreat practice. It is also the schedule of Day Sixty-Seven or Day Two Hundred and Eighty-Three.

It's valuable, if you are repeating Day Two, to read all the instructions and all the questions again. In my experience over my years of practice, every once in a while a teacher would give an instruction and I would think, "That's a *terrific* instruction. They should have given that instruction before. If they'd given that before, I would have been way ahead of where I am now." The truth is, they always had. As my understanding broadened, my capacity to understand the instruction increased. That will probably happen to you, too.

If you're leaving your retreat tomorrow, proceed to Day Three. Day Three provides the instructions for the last day of retreat, whenever that happens.

PART FOUR

Day Three

Going Home Day

Before Breakfast

Regardless of the length of a retreat, the last day has certain special characteristics. One special challenge is keeping the attention on *any* present activity. The mind leaps ahead in planning and anticipating the homecoming. For your pre-breakfast sitting meditation, you can use the awareness of this forward action of the mind as the focus of your attention.

Sit as you have been, with the intention of focusing on breath, or body sensations, or sounds—the reality of your current experience. Try to be alert to the periodic presence of the thoughts "I'm going home soon" or "I wonder if I should pack now or later." The thoughts themselves are not a problem. They are natural on moving day.

Mindfulness of these thoughts will enable you to notice them without getting involved. You can't go home before you go home, and the time you choose for packing is probably irrelevant.

Eating Meditation

A fundamental goal of practice is seeing clearly three basic truths of life: the truth of impermanence, the truth of the cause and the end of suffering, and the truth of interconnectedness–the nonseparate self. We can see all those truths in the breath. We can see all those truths in the sensations of the body. We can see all those truths in the coming and going of thoughts and feelings. We can see all those truths in eating breakfast.

I'd like to suggest that for an eating meditation you eat slowly, following all the technical instructions for eating: prepare the food slowly, eat it slowly, taste it fully. But in addition to following these technical instructions, you might try to use reflections on these three characteristics of experience as the lens through which you view your eating experience.

For example, you might think about all the ways in which impermanence manifests in eating breakfast. Before you eat, you are hungry. After you eat, you're not hungry anymore. Before you eat, there's a whole plate of food in front of you. After you eat, it's all gone. As you reflect during your breakfast on the fact that this is the last day of your retreat, you might for a moment recall how just two days ago the whole retreat stretched out in front of you. Now the whole retreat is behind you. Where did it go? It's vanished. You can't find any part of it. It's in the same past as the birth of Mozart and the voyage of the Mayflower.

If you think about the events coming up next in your life–returning home, going back to work–you realize these are all thoughts about a mythical future that seems to be moving toward you and that will soon seem to have moved behind you, just as this whole retreat experience seemed to be in front of you and now seems behind you.

Your breakfast experience can also provide the insight that suffering is caused by clinging and that the end of suffering is the result of nonclinging. Perhaps you feel a bit dismayed to be leaving, because you've been enjoying yourself. The discomfort you feel is caused by clinging to an experience that can't continue. Perhaps, on the other hand, you are eager to leave, because you are looking forward to being with certain people in your life. The eagerness is also uncomfortable. You realize that attachment to being somewhere other than here creates suffering in the mind right now. Even the tension of relatively neutral planning feels different from fully enjoying what is happening right now. In those moments in which you are able to simply relax and enjoy your breakfast, you realize the truth of the end of suffering. Whenever clinging and aversion are absent from the mind, you experience free-dom. You can eat this breakfast in total freedom.

You can also reflect on the third truth of all experi-ence–the truth of interconnectedness, the truth of the nonseparate self. Certainly on the level of physical bodies, we are separate selves. We each return to our own home and our own story and our own network of people. On the other hand, we can step back from our individual stories and realize how incredibly interconnected all life is.

Look at the food on the plate in front of you. Think about all the people who were involved in providing your breakfast, people who grew it or manufactured it or pack-aged it or delivered it–and the environment that sustained it. The fact that the food is in front of you is the sum of all the conditions that created that food. Likewise, the fact that *you* are where you are at this moment is a result of all the conditions that created you and sustained you and al-lowed you to be exactly where you are now. There are moments when it becomes absolutely clear that the entire history of the earth, probably the history of the cosmos, needed to be exactly the way it was in order for you to be exactly where you are now, eating your breakfast.

Try to eat in a relaxed way, listening to the sounds around you, enjoying the feel of your retreat space around you, enjoying your food, enjoying being right where you are at this moment.

Precept Meditation

Typically, a mindfulness retreat includes a recitation of the five traditional guidelines for wise living that the Buddha taught. I often teach these guidelines as one precept–the intention to cultivate clarity that manifests as kindness and compassion.

I like teaching about precepts at the end of a retreat when people are about to resume their regular lives. Precepts aren't mysterious; they are, for me, the way that whatever wisdom I have shows itself in my relationships with other people. A clear mind is a prerequisite for preceptful living.

I began to learn about the relationship between a clear mind and wise living twenty-three years ago while teaching hatha yoga at the College of Marin. I taught from four in the afternoon until seven every evening. When I told people about my teaching schedule, they'd say, "Isn't that a hard time for you to get out of your house?" because I had four young children at home. They'd say, "That's the busiest time of day for mothers. How do you do it?"

In fact, it *was* difficult, because I needed to get my children home from school and installed doing their homework, or delivered to the swim team, or whatever it was that they were doing, before I could leave for class. I often had the experience of running out the door internally fuming: "He should have gotten home earlier! . . . He should have remembered the homework so he didn't have to go back to school to get it! . . . He never listens!" Sometimes I would leave having had words with somebody, if only in my mind, about what they should have done differently.

I'd begin the class thinking to myself, "This is not a good way to begin to teach a hatha yoga class–all upset." But neither was it appropriate or helpful to tell my students, "My mind is all in a flurry." So I needed to wing it or fake it for the first fifteen minutes. I'd begin my yoga exercises, essentially a moving mindfulness practice. I paid attention to my own experience and described it to my students so that they could practice along with me. Often, I would be saying, "Bring your arms out to either side, pay attention to all the sensations in your arms, in your hands, and in your shoulders . . ." and I'd be thinking, "He'd better remember the homework tomorrow" while I continued, saying, ". . . move your arms back down, feel every sensation in your arms, take a breath in and out."

If I practiced diligently, I discovered that very soon I would feel as if a knot in my mind had untied itself. From nowhere would come the understanding, "He's eight years old! He doesn't care about homework. He hasn't got the concept of my teaching at the College of Marin. Let him be. He's doing fine." I would genuinely understand.

On the way to that understanding, my mind had been confused. "I'll be late. I won't do a good job. I'll appear unreliable." Fear confuses the mind. When we are calm and we pay attention, we begin to see in a wise way.

The word *wisdom* can sound formidable—as if it meant the wisdom of the ages, or amazing wisdom about how the cosmos is put together. I think that wisdom means simply knowing that things are the way they are. Eight-year-olds are just like eight-year-olds. When we are wise, we see things clearly and choose wholesome responses. Paying attention is what makes the difference.

If you like, for this period of precept meditation, think about the people in your life with whom you will be interacting this afternoon and tomorrow and in the days to come.

Preparation for Lovingkindness Meditation

The warm-up exercise for sending lovingkindness (*metta*) wishes to yourself is to think of anything valuable you ever did. The Buddha taught that the proximal cause for the arousal of *metta* is seeing the goodness in someone. Doing a mindfulness retreat is a valuable action, and you just *did* it. Buddhists might say you accumulated "merit."

At the end of a retreat, I often felt elated in an Outward Bound, I-can't-believe-I-crossed-that-chasm-by-myself-on-a-rope way. That was especially true in the early days of my practice, when retreats felt to me like visits to Space Mountain, the Disneyland indoor roller coaster. Once the ride begins, you can't get off until the end. What's more, because it's dark and you can't see the curves and loops and swerves, there is no way to anticipate them and prepare for them. There is no alternative to surrendering to the situation and riding it out. However this retreat has been for you, you've just ridden it out.

Early on, I gave up anticipating what my retreat experience was going to be. Once, in the best of moods, I filed into a meditation hall with thirty or forty other people just before we took the silence vow that marks the beginning of a retreat. Len, walking beside me, greeted me and said, "By the way, Sylvia, has your daughter gotten a job yet?"

"No," I replied, "Not yet. She's still looking."

"Radio is hard to get into," he offered, probably as a consolation, and we entered together into the silence.

The room was quiet, but my mind leaped into high-speed, self-recriminating chatter. "How could you have been such a bad mother! You should never have encouraged her! Show business is so precarious! It's probably your own dramatic impulse, projected on her! Why didn't you insist she have a *regular* career? Maybe you should sneak out of the retreat to phone her, to tell her to change careers! Len is *in* radio, he surely knows!" I was experiencing a major hindrance attack—doubtful, angry, fretful, confusing thoughts that I wished *devoutly* would go away. I don't recall when the thought tirade stopped or whether the thoughts continued until the end of the retreat. *I* stayed until the end of the retreat. I felt heroic.

As I became more knowledgeable about practice, the Space Mountain feeling subsided. Some retreats were easy, some were difficult. I realized that the intention to be mindful was what counted. Ranking experiences according to degree of difficulty is irrelevant. It's all just experience.

However your experience has been, credit yourself with merit.

Question

*But I don't feel meritorious. In fact, during
my meditation time here, I've become aware
of several things I've done that I don't feel
good about and some things I should have
done that I overlooked.*

Something that characteristically happens to me during
periods of retreat practice is that I recall, quite spontaneously, actions I regret. It's one of the things that I have
come to accept, respect, and *even* enjoy about meditation
practice.

It turns out that a spontaneous personal moral inventory is one of the consequences of the mind settling down.
When it began to happen to me, I was surprised and a little disappointed. It was demoralizing, initially, to realize
how often I made mistakes and hurt people's feelings, left
good works undone, was not totally responsive or compassionate. On the other hand, it was reassuring to discover that practice alerts me to these mistakes so that I
can make amends.

On retreat, I need to relax about the fact that I am not
able to repair my mistakes immediately. I don't write on
retreat, but I do keep a list of reparations I will make when
I return home. That way, I don't need to memorize them.

The moral inventory and my resolve to make amends
is my proof that the practice works. I believe this is what

the texts mean when they talk about practice as "the purification of the heart."

Take some moments now to sit quietly, relax, and take some intentionally long, calming breaths. Then turn the page for lovingkindness instructions.

Formal Lovingkindness Practice

The traditional ritual for ending a mindfulness retreat is a period of formal lovingkindness (*metta*) practice. Lovingkindness meditation is a structured formula for benevolent well-wishing. Initially, I thought that the reason it was the formal retreat closing practice was that it was presumed that everyone would be in a relaxed and happy mood. Wishing well to all beings, including yourself, is an obvious, natural reflection of feeling good. I now believe that wishing well to yourself (and all beings) is also the most compassionate response to *not* feeling good, as well as its most natural antidote. So whatever your situation is, end with some lovingkindness.

Sit in a comfortable place, in a comfortable position. Close your eyes and feel yourself breathing. Think of someone whom you love a lot, someone who you think loves you a lot. In traditional texts this person is called "the benefactor," because we feel grateful to have such a person in our lives.

The thought of such a beloved person brings delight to the mind. It's easy to send them warm wishes. You can make up whatever words you want to express your wishes. Very simple, traditional words are

> *May you be happy.*
> *May you be peaceful.*

Say the phrases over and over to yourself in your mind. Many people find it helpful to say one phrase on the "in" breath and one on the "out" breath. It isn't necessary to limit yourself to the "one breath-one phrase" mode, but you might want to try this method to see if it helps keep your attention focused.

It's quite likely that thinking warm thoughts toward a benefactor will help you think similar thoughts toward yourself. I believe that's why the Buddha suggested that sending good wishes to yourself ought to come second after sending them to someone whom you love tremendously. That way, regardless of how you may be feeling toward yourself, the energy of your connection with your cherished person erases any hesitation you might have about wishing yourself well. Use the same phrases:

> *May I be peaceful.*
> *May I be happy.*

For a few minutes, try alternating sets of phrases—one set for your well-beloved, one set for yourself. Try to practice with wholehearted intention, with the sense that well-wishing matters, but don't get tense about it. Lovingkindness is happy practice. Smile.

After a while, whenever you feel ready, think of other people you know and love. Often, people report that the very moment they decide to include someone other than their "benefactor," a long line of other people immediately assembles in the mind to wait their turn to receive blessings. You can linger with the image of particular individuals for a while, or you can move through your lineup, one wish per person. The phrases stay the same:

May you be peaceful.
May you be happy.

A further step in formal practice is bringing to mind images of people with whom you have had difficulties. When the mind is relaxed from wishing well to well-loved people, it sometimes manages to *stay* relaxed even when it fills with thoughts of not-well-loved people. If you want to try the difficult person category for a few minutes, go ahead. The phrases are the same:

May you be happy.
May you be peaceful.

You'll know if you were ready to move on to this more challenging category. If you thought, "I still remember what this person did to me, and I wish he hadn't—but I don't need to wish him ill," then you were ready.

If you thought, "Oh dear, I wish I hadn't reminded myself of this person—now I'm becoming upset because I remember what she did to me," you'll know that it wasn't time yet to include her. Moving on can wait for another day. Go back to thinking about your benefactor. Or go through your line of good friends. Or wish yourself well again until your upset feelings disappear.

Whenever you want to, you can continue your lovingkindness practice in walking mode. Weather permitting, go outside. Take a walk on a larger scale than your small walking path, one that is likely to include face-to-face encounters with other beings. If you've done your retreat in a city setting, you'll probably pass lots of people as you walk. If you've been in the country, perhaps you'll pass only sheep and cows. If you have done a wilderness retreat, you may see birds or butterflies. The important common denominator shared by people and cows and birds is that they are all living beings. An especially lovely line of the *Metta Sutta*, the Buddha's teaching on lovingkindness practice, is "May all beings be happy, whatever their living nature."

Walk for half an hour—more if you want to and if the circumstances permit—and wish well to every living being you encounter. If wishing cows happiness seems silly, you can modify the phrases. You can say:

May you be well.
May you be well.
May you be well . . .

Every so often, remember to say:

May I be well.

The ultimate goal of lovingkindness practice is replacing particular well-wishing with universal well-wishing in which all beings are held equally dear. Reciting the traditional *metta* phrases for all beings inclines the mind in this direction. Finish your walk with global vision, seeing everything and choosing nothing.

May all beings be happy.
May all beings be peaceful.

"The Important Thing Is to Plant"

Whatever your retreat experience was, it was enough. There is absolutely no way of evaluating mindfulness practice on the spot. Feeling ecstatic, or even feeling good, is not necessarily a criterion. There are lots of ways to temporarily alter experience that aren't necessarily conducive to wisdom. On the other hand, if you are finishing your retreat feeling saddened, that's not necessarily a sign that you did it wrong. Maybe you learned an important truth that you've been hiding from yourself. That would be progress.

If you feel relaxed, that's great. But if you don't, even if you feel unnerved, it could mean you are on the *way* to some new understanding. You never know. Perhaps you are thinking, "Oh, I'm just now catching on to how every moment arises and disappears, and now I have to go home!" Every moment arises and disappears at home just the same as on retreat. You can go home.

My friend Sharon describes mindfulness practice by using the image of a farmer sowing a field of seeds. She says, "Seeds get thrown all over the place. Some sprout immediately, and others, because the soil isn't warm enough or wet enough, sprout later." I used to hear

Sharon's image in terms of my own garden. I'd think of the things I routinely did to prepare the soil. Meditation practice seems like ongoing soil preparation.

A big part of practice is *intention*. In traditional texts, intention is discussed as "inclining the mind in the direction of insight." I believe that the very act of setting aside time to practice mindfulness, just *doing* it, "inclines the mind."

My friend Mary Kay phoned this morning. I told her I couldn't plant my usual big garden this year because I'm writing as fast as I can to meet a book deadline. I said, "I don't have time for a full-out garden this year. I've just put in some tomatoes and some zucchini."

"That's okay," Mary Kay replied. "The important thing is to plant."

The Great Gift
of Mindfulness

When I teach people mindfulness, I usually explain to them that it is scientific. I tell them the Buddha was a terrific psychologist and that he offered a wonderfully straightforward explanation for how the mind works. I often say, "Mindfulness is practical. Being present in every single moment with full understanding and calm acceptance is a contented, happy way to live. It makes sense. It's entirely rational. It's not magic."

That's not quite the whole story. At the beginning of this retreat, I suggested that mindfulness was a way of being wise and becoming wise at the same time. I want to end by saying that practice over time is a way of becoming more and *more* wise. Mindfulness is the practice that the Buddha taught for becoming a fully wise, compassionate, loving, and happy person.

According to the Buddha, enlightened people have perfected ten special qualities. They are called *paramitas*. Here is the list: morality, resolve, renunciation, effort, equanimity, truthfulness, patience, lovingkindness, generosity, and wisdom.

Think back over your retreat experience. I see the intention to do retreat practice, even before the retreat begins, as an act of *morality,* a reflection of our desire to be kind to ourselves and others. You needed *resolve* to carry out the retreat, and being away from friends and family and normal routine for these retreat days required *renunciation* and *effort.* Each time you accommodated to a new situation, a new feeling, or a new thought, you practiced *equanimity.* Every moment of alert presence was a moment of *truthfulness.* Staying on retreat was an act of *patience.* Offering *lovingkindness* was an act of *generosity.* Understanding that was a sign of *wisdom.* You did it all. Just with mindfulness.

I once saw TV news coverage of a special triathlon for cooking school students. Instead of bike–run–swim, the events were bike–run–cook! Each competitor, after being issued a rucksack with mystery contents at the starting line, biked the requisite number of miles and then ran the requisite distance, carrying the pack all the way. At the end of the run, they all arrived at a huge kitchen full of stoves, and everyone cooked up the contents of their rucksack. Everyone's sack contained identical ingredients.

The ingredients for becoming like a Buddha are part of our basic character potential.

The cooking school students *knew* they were cooking. Unbeknownst to you, while you were sitting and walking and paying attention, the ten *paramitas* were simmering, all by themselves. Think of their cultivation as the great gift of mindfulness.

Cooking Buddha Soup

Ingredients:

> *Morality*
>
> *Resolve*
>
> *Renunciation*
>
> *Effort*
>
> *Equanimity*
>
> *Truthfulness*
>
> *Patience*
>
> *Lovingkindness*
>
> *Generosity*
>
> *Wisdom*

Method of Preparation:

> *Apply equal amounts of concentration, calm, equanimity, rapture, investigation, energy, and mindfulness.*
>
> *Enjoy.*

Resources

For more information about Insight Meditation, contact:

Spirit Rock Meditation Center
5000 Sir Francis Drake Blvd., Box 909C
Woodacre, CA 94973
(415) 488-0164

Insight Meditation Society
1230 Pleasant Street, Barre, MA 01005
(508) 355-4378

Tapes and books are available through:

Dharma Seed Tape Library
PO Box 66, Wendell Depot, MA 01380
(800) 969-7333

Other retreat books available from Harper San Francisco:

The Recollected Heart: A Monastic Retreat with Philip Zaleski

Renewing Your Soul: A Guided Retreat for the Sabbath and Other Days of Rest with David A. Cooper

About the Author

Sylvia Boorstein teaches mindfulness and leads retreats across the United States. She is a co–founding teacher (with Jack Kornfield) at the Spirit Rock Meditation Center in Woodacre, California, and a senior teacher at the Insight Meditation Society in Barre, Massachusetts. Boorstein is also a practicing psychotherapist. She is the author of *It's Easier Than You Think: The Buddhist Way to Happiness.*